GLACIER TRAVEL
◆ AND ◆
CREVASSE RESCUE

ANDY SELTERS

The Mountaineers/Seattle

The Mountaineers: Organized 1906 *"...to explore, study, preserve, and enjoy the natural beauty of the Northwest."*

4 3
5 4 3

Published by The Mountaineers
1011 S.W. Klickitat Way, Suite 107 Seattle, WA 98134
Published simultaneously in Canada by Douglas & McIntyre, Ltd.,
    1615 Venables Street, Vancouver, B.C. V5L 2H1
Published simultaneously in Great Britain by Diadem/Hodder & Stoughton, London

Manufactured in the United States of America
Edited by Nicholas Allison
Illustrations by Jennifer Hahn
Cover design by Bridget Culligan
Book design by Bridget Culligan
Front cover: Climber on Choktoi Glacier below the Ogre, Karakoram, Pakistan. Back cover: Party on Kahiltna Glacier, Mount McKinley, Alaska. Photos by Alan Kearney.
Photos on pages 2 and 134 by Bob and Ira Spring. All other photos by the author.
Frontispiece: Crevasse on the Cowlitz Glacier, Mount Rainier, Washington; Mount Adams in the distance.

Library of Congress Cataloging in Publication Data
Selters, Andrew.
    Glacier travel and crevasse rescue / by Andy Selters.
        p.   cm.
    Includes bibliographical references and index.
    ISBN 0-89886-250-7
    1. Snow and ice climbing.   2. Snow and ice climbing—Safety measures.   3. Mountaineering—Search and rescue operations.   I. Mountaineers (Society)   II. Title.
GV200.3.S45   1990   90-37685
796.5'22'0289—dc20   CIP

Contents

6

Acknowledgments

I inherited the concept of this book from DAVE BISHOP, former guide for the North Cascades Alpine School. In the many years and many revisions since Dave left the project for medical school, a number of others have helped me develop this text. Of those, BRIAN OKONEK of Alaska-Denali Guiding provided valuable information from the standpoint of an expert in Alaskan mountaineering. Others who helped were coworkers of mine at the American Alpine Institute; JOHN SCHUTT offered an especially wide range of helpful suggestions, glaciologist RON JOHNSON added his expertise to the hazard evaluation chapter, and JILL FUGATE helped edit early drafts. TOM DICKEY, BRUCE HENDRICKS, MARK HOUSTON, ALAN KEARNEY, DR. ERIC LARSON, LANCE MACHOVSKY and ROBERT PARKER all had answers to various queries, as did pack maker RICK LIPKE of Skagit Mountain Rescue. Finally, thanks to JENNIFER HAHN for her patience and creativity in developing the illustrations.

Andy Selters
Bellingham, Washington

Party of climbers in the 1920s on a ladder ascent of a crevasse wall, Mount Rainier, Washington. (Photo courtesy of the National Park Service)

ties, skiing with sleds, traveling on large, remote glaciers with rotten snow conditions.

While advances in awareness and technique can make glacier travel quite a bit safer and more efficient, they can never reach perfection, so each traveler must compromise as he sees fit. In this book enough procedure is described to satisfy the safety conscious, and those who are more interested in speed can compromise as they wish.

In that sense, this book should not be considered a final statement but a reference on which to build your own experiences. Also, discussion and controversy need to continue, for refinements in technique will result. While this text integrates techniques from climbers around the world, a bias toward the techniques familiar to the American Pacific Northwest is inevitable. The reader is presumed to have basic mountaineering skills, particularly the basic knots and techniques for self-arrest, rappelling, and belaying. Beginners can find these skills described in a general mountaineering text, and should seek competent instruction in them.

In any case, as with any physical skill, reading alone does not produce proficiency. Glacier travel problems are impromptu engineering problems, with materials and time crucially limited and no certainty of the forces involved. The keys to competence are snow savvy, practice in roped travel and rescue techniques, a constant, critical evaluation of situations, and a bit of a sixth sense. We achieve these only through applying "book knowledge" to years of excursions and on mock (or actual) rescues. Therefore, beginners and those of intermediate experience are especially warned to err on the side of caution whenever there is a question.

The most fundamental principle underlying this book is that any party on a glacier must assume that, in a mishap, either they themselves will be the rescuers or there will be no rescue. Accepting this total self-sufficiency is not only the best possible incentive to be competent and prepared, it's also a responsibility to organized rescue teams and nearby parties, who may or may not be available in time to risk their own goals and lives in a rescue. Thus, the bottom line reads that self-sufficiency is a responsibility. And after all, being self-sufficient in the mountains is really the essence of the "freedom of the hills."

CHAPTER 1

UNDERSTANDING THE CREVASSE HAZARD

Glaciers vary widely in the number of crevasses they hide, and their surface conditions change constantly. Therefore, the danger of breaking through a snowbridge into a crevasse ranges from negligible to very high, depending on the glacier and its condition. Just leaving camp on an Alaskan glacier in bad conditions can be riskier than climbing for two days on a typical alpine glacier. On the other hand, occasional treacherous conditions can make an alpine glacier just as dangerous as one in Alaska.

Obviously, one would like to know just how hazardous a given place is at a given time. However, beyond recognizing obvious open crevasses, "knowing" the crevasse hazard generally amounts to making educated guesses and using a lot of intuition. The starting point toward making your guesses more educated and your intuition more practiced is to understand the origins of glaciers and crevasses.

Glacier and
Crevasse Genesis

Glaciers form in the world's high and cold places where, during the average year, more snow falls than can melt away. Decade after decade the snow piles on top of itself, and as it does so the older, deeply buried layers gradually compact into ice. Eventually the mass of snow-ice grows large enough to sag (with internal deformation) and slide downhill. It's this characteristic of MOVEMENT that mostly defines a glacier.

Continuously fed by the deepening snows at a glacier's head, glacier ice imperceptibly creeps down to lower elevations, where temperate summers dissipate it into meltwater. Thus, geologists often look at a glacier as a gravity-driven system that dissipates "excess" snowfall. The upper area, where more snow falls than can melt away, is called the ACCUMULATION ZONE. The lower area, where the accumulated ice that has moved down from above melts away, is called the ABLATION ZONE. In late summer and autumn, when a year's melting is nearly complete, you can often easily distinguish the white, still-snowy accumulation zone from the old blue-gray ice of the ablation zone.

Glacier ice behaves much differently than the rigid, brittle stuff of cocktail parties and hockey rinks; with tons of more recent ice and snow weighing on it, glacier ice flows almost like a viscous lava, speeding and stretching, slowing and pooling, turning and flexing with the terrain in a slow plastic creep. But while the supercompressed majority of ice within a glacier can ooze through the terrain this way, the ice closer to the surface is more brittle. Thus, when moving ice strains to flow over bedrock features, the brittle surface cracks, something like the way an old rubber band splits when it's stretched. These cracks in the glacier's surface are crevasses.

Most crevasses form in TENSION ZONES, where ice moving faster stretches away from ice moving slower. The tension zones easiest to visualize are those where the gradient steepens, where the ice accelerates down the steeper slope and tends to pull away from the ice on the more gentle slope above (see fig. 1.1). This tension creates TRANSVERSE crevasses, slots that form perpendicular to the glacier's flow. A smooth drop will make a series of parallel crevasses from a bit above the dropoff to somewhere above the bottom. At the bottom of the dropoff, in simplistic theory anyway, the crevasses are sealed shut by the pooling, compressive flow, and this area is known as a COMPRESSION ZONE.

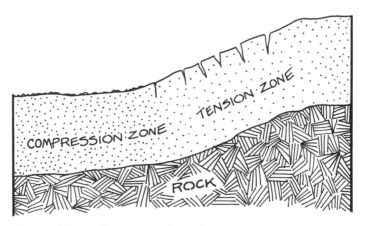

Figure 1.1   Cross-section of tension and compression zones

Crevasse-forming tension also occurs where a glacier's margins drag and press against the adjacent mountain slopes and valley walls. Here the center of a glacier is less affected, and a central stream of ice courses on faster and more freely, as in the leading arm of an amoeba. This puts two forces on the glacier's margins: compression from the adjoining rock, and tension from the faster central stream. Classi-

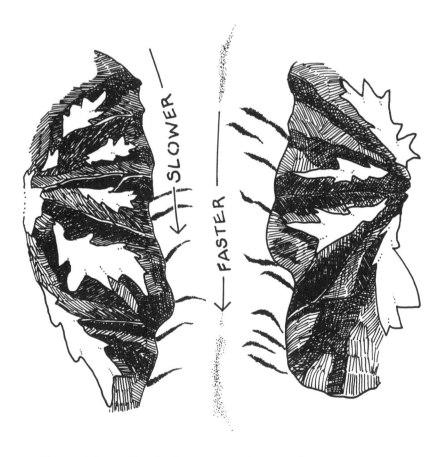

Figure 1.2   Marginal crevasses *(top view)*

cally these forces combine to create a pattern of herringbone crevasses angling up-glacier at 45 degrees, as shown in figure 1.2. These are called MARGINAL crevasses. An element of this "marginal drag" often flexes transverse crevasses into crescent shapes. Marginal friction is to some degree present along most of a glacier's length, and therefore the freer-flowing center usually offers a more crevasse-free area to travel in.

Turns generate tension as well. The ice on the outside of a turn has farther to travel and thus is pulled with tension, creating RADIAL crevasses. On the other hand, ice along the inside edge decelerates and, for reasons not well understood, apparently spreads. This spreading force forms crisscross crevasses. Similar forces create chaotic crevasses where glaciers from different drainages converge. Where the two streams jam together the ice slows, and their central streams pull away to create jumbles of marginal crevasses. Compressive forces from the merging glaciers complicate the situation, on the one hand sealing up the crevasses, but also creating pressure that speeds up the flow, helping to create crevasses.

Where a glacier spills into a broader valley or plain it spreads laterally, and this spreading can form LONGITUDINAL crevasses, which run parallel to a glacier's general flow. In our era most glaciers in the world flow off mountains into drainages that were widened by much larger glaciers during the Pleistocene Epoch. Thus many of today's glaciers spread as they flow into these broadened drainages, creating longitudinal crevasses near their termini.

In heavily glaciated regions like the Alaska Range, the tops of ridges can accumulate enough snow and ice to initiate flow off either side of the ridge line, creating a tension zone atop the ridge. Thus crevasses can form along broad, relatively flat ridges. Those used to windswept ridge tops in a moderately glaciated region like the Cascades never expect to see crevasses here. In an analogous situation, the perennial cornices along ridge tops in heavily glaciated terrain can teeter downslope at glacial slowness, leaving shallow crevasses as they slowly crack away from the ridge line.

Finally, there is the uppermost crevasse in a glacier, the BERGSCHRUND (see fig. 1.3). This is the gap where the glacier pulls away from stationary ice and snow above. Above most bergschrunds there rises a steeper mountain head-wall that sloughs off most snowfall, a headwall too steep to collect enough mass to become part of the moving glacier. Because of all the snow that fills in from this headwall above, bergschrunds generally aren't as deep as normal crevasses, although they can be enormously wide and long.

Cousins to bergschrunds are MOATS, the melt-gaps between a glacier's edge and its surrounding rock walls. Moats can be fatally deep and can be overhung by weak

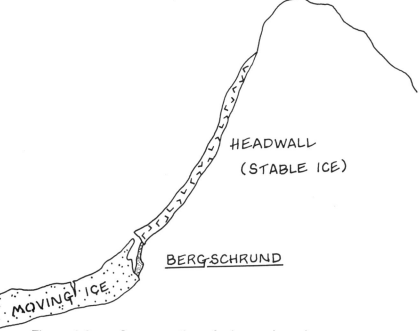

Figure 1.3   Cross-section of a bergschrund

snow just like a crevasse. With solid ground so near, it's easy to overlook moats, but they must be approached with the same caution as crevasses. Often rock anchors must be placed to belay across a moat.

As to the form of crevasses, most are generally linear, but their size ranges from hairline slits to gigantic chasms capable of swallowing entire neighborhoods. Larger, thicker glaciers and the colder glaciers of the polar regions have larger and deeper crevasses. Glaciologists differ as to just how deep crevasses can get, but most reckon it's a rare crevasse that's much deeper than 100 feet (except in polar regions), even though legends claim that many are deeper. Because glacier ice's plasticity increases gradually with depth, crevasses tend to narrow gradually with their depth as well. Thus a common fate of those who fall far into one is getting tightly wedged.

The more active a glacier, the more crevasses it generates, so that small, stagnating glaciers essentially are snowfields with a bergschrund and a crevasse or two, while active sections of large glaciers might have more crevasses than solid ground in between. Many glaciers spill over cliffs or very steep sections, and here the ice periodically calves off in hunks of various proportions. The resulting chaos of crevasses and towers (called SERACS) is known as an ICEFALL.

This outline gives us a general idea of glacier flow and how crevasses form, but, as with fluid studies in general, science has never fully comprehended the dynamics of glaciers. Combinations of dropping, turning, dragging, colliding, pooling, and so on can create crevasses angling in any direction. Also, a glacier's flow will often deform crevasses as it carries them out of their original tension zone. However, whatever the combined forces, in a given zone on a glacier the forces tend to be similar, and therefore it's common to find crevasses within a given area running fairly parallel to one another (see fig. 1.4).

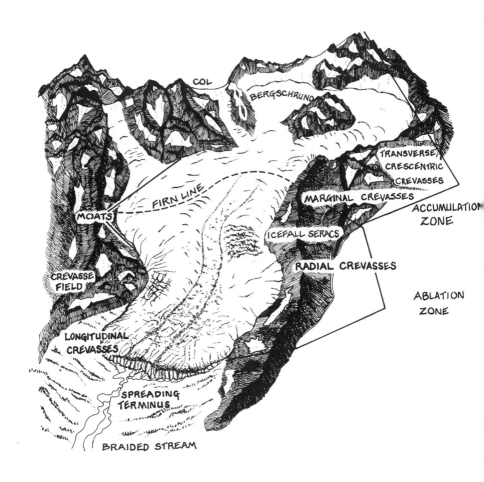

Figure 1.4   Glacier overview

Snowbridges

The above discussion gives the glacier traveler an abstract idea of where crevasses are most likely to be found, but it's the snow that bridges crevasses unpredictably that makes them dangerous. Thus, the most important clues to judging the crevasse hazard are a sharp eye for the dips and extensions of snowbridges, and an understanding of and subtle feel for the changing strength of snow underfoot.

One characteristic of snow is that it tends to stick together. The "glue" is simply tiny necks of ice that freeze the individual crystals into an intricate network. Thus, when snow falls on a crevassed glacier, instead of dribbling into the crevasses like sand, many of the crystals accrete onto the crevasse lips, especially if the temperature is not far below freezing and if there is a wind. In this way cornices build out from the edges, and eventually these meet and partially or entirely bridge the crevasse.

When snowbridges are strong, they allow mercifully straightforward travel over crevasse-riddled terrain. But when they're weak, they unexpectedly drop climbers into crevasses' dark depths. Whether a bridge gives the boon of access or the bane of collapse depends partly on its thickness, but more on the strength of its bonding network. With the nearly infinite types of snow, from new-fallen powder to old wind crust, this bonding network can be amazingly strong or hopelessly weak. The interacting forces of temperature, humidity, solar radiation, wind, and snow's own weight determine snow's characteristics; so the strength of an untrodden snowbridge is a direct result of the climatic history and the present weather.

Because of the seasonal pattern of most climates, most snowbridges are seasonal affairs. In most regions they form and thicken during a stormy season, and then they progressively collapse during the fair-weather season, the season that climbers naturally favor. Let's take a closer look now at the main processes affecting snow, and hence snowbridges.

Newly fallen snow is rather weak, but, as a general rule, as soon as the delicate crystals land they start to settle, and the accumulated layer gradually strengthens. Compaction, sintering (rounding of crystals due to vapor transfer), and wind-battering—collectively known as "age-hardening"—all combine to consolidate the originally intricate, individual snowflakes into small, rounded grains held together by stronger, more interconnected bonds (see fig. 1.5). This process goes on in temperatures below the melting point, although it slows to insignificance below –40 degrees Fahrenheit or so. Thus, within a couple of days to a couple of weeks after falling, snow usually strengthens considerably. Deeper snow will compress and strengthen itself more, so that thicker snowbridges are stronger not only from their greater mass but from a sturdier bonding network as well.

When this "new" (unmelted) snow, whether well settled or not, first warms to the melting point (generally in the spring), the bonding network quickly collapses. In the first thaws, the necks between crystals melt first, and the snow can swiftly deteriorate into an insubstantial slurry of crystals and meltwater. The low-density, dry snow of continental and subarctic regions has weaker bonds that break down faster and more deeply than those of the denser, already wetter snow of maritime climates. But in any case, when the meltwater refreezes (generally at night) the bonds re-form more thickly, the crystals grow larger and rounder, and the whole network consolidates, stronger than before. What typically happens then, during late springtime, is that daytime heat melts the snowbridges into weak slush, and then nighttime cold freezes them into strong "Styrofoam-snow," or melt-freeze (MF) snow. When the melt-freeze cycles continue for many weeks the snow gradually consolidates into very coarse-grained, very firm snow known as FIRN. Daytime heat softens only the very surface of firn,

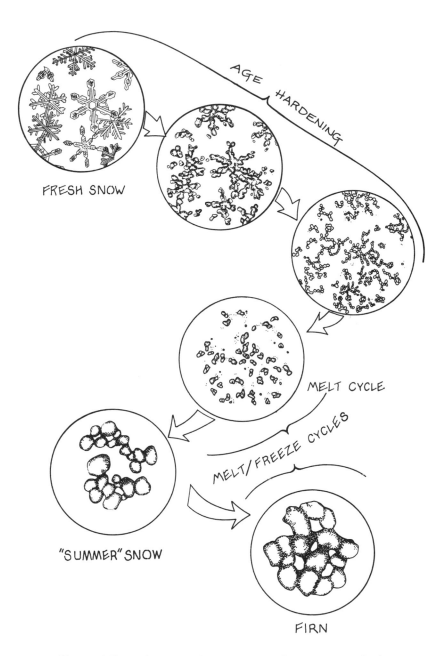

Figure 1.5   Important processes of snow on a glacier

and even a plunging ice-ax shaft might penetrate just a few inches.

For the typical summer excursion, then, it can be invaluable to get a feel for the strength of snow after a given period of melt-freeze cycles, and to continually assess a day's ongoing cycle.

Besides gauging the general snow conditions, one of course wants to know exactly where the hidden crevasses lie. This is difficult when snowbridges are of "new" snow, for unmelted snow tends to cover a glacier's structure with a smooth, level blanket. But after a bridge goes through some melt-freeze cycles it begins to sag. With time these sags can become quite dramatic. Also, as spring goes on, the low-lying sags tend to collect more dust. In a late-spring or summer dusting of snow they also tend to collect more of the new powder. Thus it's common to see snow-bridges accentuated by dustier snow or, conversely, by cleaner, whiter snow.

Also, when snowbridges collapse they rarely do so all at once. Rather, sections of the bridge progressively melt and drop away, leaving a hole that hints at a wider and longer underlying crevasse. So when you see a hole in the glacier's surface it's wise to assume there's a crevasse extending well beyond the visible abyss, especially lengthwise.

Even though many crevasses do give some visual clues to their existence, many others do not. The history of mountaineering includes the obituaries of many who found this out the hard way. The prudent assume that anywhere there's snow on a glacier there might be a crevasse.

Glacier "Seasons" in Various Climates

Knowing the patterns of snow evolution, now we can generalize the typical annual cycles of surface conditions on glaciers of various climates.

MARITIME, TEMPERATE CLIMATES

Most glacier travel goes on in temperate latitudes, in mountain areas with generally winter-wet and summer-dry climates like the Cascades, and the European and New Zealand alps.

Winter in the temperate latitudes is characterized by a westerly storm track that buries glaciers with deep snowfall. Mountain slopes near the west coasts of the continents receive a particularly heavy load of wet, maritime snowfall. Slightly more continental, the Alps receive somewhat less winter snow than the Cascades. Aside from meaning a lot of poor weather to travel in, midwinter's heavy snows present glacier travelers with good news and bad news. The bad news is that under the deep, unmelted snow most crevasses are undetectable, and secondly, since temperatures persist below the freezing point, the snow cannot melt and refreeze into a stronger network. The good news is that although crevasses are hidden, most bridges become thick enough to bear plenty of weight. Thus, most climbers consider the typical middle to late temperate winter to be a relatively safe time to travel, especially on skis. (See fig. 1.6 for complete snowbridge cycle.)

This relative safety continues until sometime in the spring, when long days, a high sun and warm air start melting the snowpack. Depending on the depth of the pack and the heat of the season, within a week or two the bridges start to sag and collapse, and become quite unsafe. Strong sun makes snowbridges most dangerous in the afternoon and evening, with nighttime freezes bringing relative safety

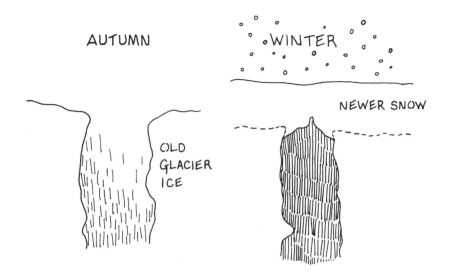

Figure 1.6   Typical snowbridge seasons on a temperate glacier

during the late night and early morning. But spring conditions can be especially treacherous if a nighttime cloud cover or generally warm air keeps the snow from refreezing at night, so that the following day meltwater percolates much deeper into the snowpack and deteriorates the bridges that much more. Down in the ablation zone the spring thaw starts early, and it gradually progresses up the glacier as the season warms further. This means that when the lower part of a glacier has its "spring," the upper reaches are still in "winter."

As spring turns to summer, the lengthening "melt" portion of the daily melt-freeze cycle collapses many snowbridges, and the crevasses open up. After a few weeks of this cyclic decay those bridges that persist withstand melt-weakening more and more, and they are more likely to remain firm into late morning or even midday. However,

SPRING   SUMMER

a late spring or early summer snowfall can treacherously rebridge the newly open crevasses with a scanty few inches of new snow. In the the cooler, higher elevations of the Pennine and Bernese alps summer snowfalls are common and many bridges persist through the season. Overall, though, warm summer weather on a temperate glacier gradually opens more crevasses, and leaves fewer but more trustworthy snowbridges and cornices. By late September on a Cascade glacier there might not be a single snowbridge left, and the primary challenge of travel can be to wend a route through mazes of wide-open crevasses. In New Zealand stormy summers maintain "winter" in the accumulation zones through to the autumn.

As temperatures drop, autumn snowfalls dangerously veil open crevasses with a thin layer of powder. As little as four or five inches of new snow can lay an even, white blanket that obscures all signs of crevasses, but of course this snow will not support the most feather-light climber. Not only is it almost certain at this time that any bridge or overhang will give way, but it can be very difficult to stop a partner's crevasse fall, for the hard summer surface underneath can be quite difficult to self-arrest on, and the stiff crevasse lip will slow the rope very little (see the travel and rescue chapters). When conditions are like this, it's wise to just stay off glaciers. Late-fall and early-winter snow accumulations, though, first make it easier to hold a partner's fall, then gradually stack the bridges high enough to bear weight, bringing a return to the relative safety of midwinter.

SUBARCTIC CLIMATES

Typified by those in the Alaska Range, subarctic glaciers receive much of their snow in the late summer and early fall. Thus, crevasses can be fairly well covered as the bitter but relatively dry winter moves in. However, winter's dry, intense cold keeps bridges from strengthening as much as on temperate glaciers. During the winter it's mostly wind that age-hardens the snow, so that exposed spots become stiff with a few inches of "wind board." Pockets protected from the wind remain powdery into the spring thaw.

When thawing temperatures arrive in April, May or June (depending on the elevation), the subarctic days are so long that meltwater suddenly percolates well into the snowpack, making it deeply treacherous for weeks. The bridges, built of cold, light snow and suddenly infused with meltwater, can show little or no sag or stress before even surprisingly thick ones collapse readily, especially in the warm afternoons. As a result climbers in the Alaska Range fall through far more frequently and more unexpectedly than they do on temperate glaciers.

Midsummer opens the crevasses and deteriorates bridges with appalling speed, but firmer, more trustworthy bridges usually don't develop, because occasional or frequent snowfalls keep renewing them with untrustworthy snow. This oscillation between thawing temperatures and accumulating snow is the ideal circumstance to prolong instability. Like any glacier condition, this prolonged instability moves up the glaciers with the season, and so unstable new bridges are a serious problem somewhere on the giant Alaskan glaciers throughout the spring and summer. Moderate to severe instability can persist until the colder days and heavier snows of late summer and autumn rebuild the bridges to relative strength.

CONTINENTAL CLIMATES

The Canadian Rockies and the eastern Alps (Bergalia and Tyrol) typify a continental climate: very cold in the winter, with snowfalls that can come any time of year. Often the winters bring only modest snowfall—just a few feet or less of dry powder—and therefore crevasse bridges can remain barely substantial into the early spring. But storms usually pass through during March through May, building bridges as the temperature gradually warms. Then, as in a maritime summer, melt-freeze cycles can alternately deteriorate and firm the snowbridges, or twenty-four-hour melting temperatures can just weaken them. Snowfall and rain are common too, and thus bridges often remain relatively soggy and treacherous, especially at higher elevations. September typically brings an early onset of cold air and more stable (although quite broken) glacier surfaces, until occasional storms bridge the fairly open slots with light powder.

SUBTROPICAL AND TROPICAL GLACIERS

The very high and extensive mountains of the Himalaya and the Andes have a wide range of climates. In general their high altitude and low latitude bring snow conditions that can fool a climber used to temperate glaciers. Snow deteriorating under an intense sun in the very dry air does not always turn slushy; rather, the moisture sublimates or evaporates. The snow structure weakens, by becoming more airy and "rotten," without the telltale sogginess of warm snow at temperate latitudes. Also, the intense radiation exaggerates the difference between north- and south-facing slopes.

In the Nepal Himalaya two distinct seasons feed the glaciers: from June to early September the summer monsoon dumps a lot of relatively wet snow at the higher elevations, and, from late December through March, winter storms drop moderate amounts of cold, dry snow. During both the pre- and postmonsoon climbing seasons, melt-freeze conditions prevail and gradually open up the crevasses. The surprisingly warm premonsoon season, right after winter's colder snowfall, can make for especially treacherous bridges. Somewhat cooler and shorter days in the postmonsoon season make the opening-up process more gradual. New snow can rebridge crevasses anytime during the two climbing seasons.

Farther northwest in the Himalaya chain, in the Karakoram, the monsoon has little effect and the continental climate brings snowfall any time of year. However, the very high elevations attract much more precipitation overall than in most continental ranges, and so the glaciers are much larger and have larger crevasses. With the spring thaw come searing hot days, but the nights remain cold. Thus, throughout summer these radical temperature swings induce radical melt-freeze cycles. Unfortunately, periodic storms between clear spells usually keep adding fresh snowfall, and therefore the accumulation zones of the Karakoram glaciers can be as treacherous as those in Alaska.

In the Andes of Peru and Bolivia one finds a much more favorable and markedly seasonal climate. The high-sun season (October through March) sees easterly trade winds bringing more or less daily snow, while the low-sun climbing season (late May through August or September) brings extensive clear weather with some afternoon squalls. During the climbing season, then, melt-freeze cycles go on predictably, opening but strengthening the glaciers' surfaces. The chance of snowstorms rebuilding soft bridges decreases farther south, and in Bolivia the dry season is particularly long and pronounced.

Climbing a glacier on Imjatse, Khumbu, Nepal

CHAPTER 2

PRINCIPLES AND PROCEDURES OF GLACIER TRAVEL

[The crevasses] soon became more numerous and were ugly things to look into, much more so to cross. . . .The snow lay up to [their] edges and travelling became so insecure that we had to take to the ropes, and so, like a long chain of criminals, we wound our way along. In this mode we moved much faster, each man taking his run and clearing even broad crevasses if they crossed the direction we were travelling.

Henry Haversham Godwin-Austen,
on exploring the Karakoram for the Mustagh Pass, 1860

I t cannot be overstated how valuable it is to under-stand crevasses and snow, in order to do your best to stay off weak snowbridges. But no one can judge snow perfectly, so for the glacier traveler the bottom line re-mains: where there's snow on a glacier there's a chance of plunging into a crevasse. Exactly how great this chance is no one can be certain, and the likelihood varies greatly with place and time. Therefore, with uncertainty as an assumption, partners on a snow-covered glacier travel roped together, with the idea that they will hold each other's crevasse falls and rescue each other. This chapter covers the procedures for travel, and the next two chapters cover rescue.

As straightforward as roped travel sounds, only co-ordinated, alert teamwork can allow a team to travel efficiently, and only with thorough preparations can they realistically have the safety net they expect; a simple "rope up and go" attitude gives only a false sense of security. To a beginner, the preparations and considerations might seem overwhelming, or to the naive they might seem like burdensome rigamarole. But after just a handful of ex-cursions the procedures become almost second nature.

Arranging Members: How Far Apart?

Glacier travel teams function differently depending on the number of members, their experience, and how they ar-range themselves on their rope(s).

Other things being equal, much of a team's dynamics hinge on how far apart members tie in and travel. A greater distance between members means there's plenty of rope to span wide crevasses, very little chance of one falling member pulling in another, and more freedom to negotiate corners and zigzags. However, greater distance between members also makes it easier to develop more slack between them, potentially enough more to deepen a trivial "punch in" into a fall requiring a rescue. With these trade-offs in mind, let's see how the different teams of two to five members work.

THREE-PERSON ROPE TEAMS

Having three people per rope, one on each end and one in the middle, has long been the accepted minimum for a glacier travel team because, assuming the members travel with care, it virtually assures that two people will be available to hold a fall and anchor the rope. With a 150- or 165-foot rope, this sets the members a relatively distant 75 to 80 feet apart. On an Alaskan or Karakoram-size glacier one wants this distance to span large crevasses, but for smaller glaciers, particularly those with complex crevasse fields, there can be an advantage to traveling with a shorter span.

In general, a shorter span has less slack, and thus crevasse falls will be shorter. In crevasse fields, shorter spans are easier to keep closer to perpendicular to the crevasses (see under "Team Travel" below). To shorten the span, the end partners can each tie in 20 to 25 feet from the rope's end and carry the slack coiled and knotted over their shoulders, or use the kiwi tie-in described in appendix 2. This "spare" rope also comes in handy during rescues.

Whether on a long or short span, members of differing abilities should arrange themselves so that the person most practiced at routefinding and judging crevasses leads, and the less experienced of the other two travels in the middle.

FOUR- TO FIVE-PERSON ROPE TEAMS

A party of four or five can choose whether to travel on one rope or two. Advantages to all four or five traveling on one rope (one on each end and the others tied in evenly along its length) include more person-power to hold falls, and less rope weight to carry per person. Too, if a party of four or five includes a couple of novices, it can be wiser to "hide" them in the middle of a single, more populous rope than to "expose" them on the end of another rope.

What a rope team of four or five needs to consider, however, is that traveling together on one rope puts them closer together (less than 40 feet apart with five on a 165-foot rope), adding some risk—usually small, but potentially significant—that two instead of just one could end up in a slot. Also, a more populous rope team will find more hassles and slower going as the members turn corners, hop crevasses, pace themselves and generally coordinate with one another. Finally, a party of four or five that divides itself into two rope teams can find the second rope giving them more options in the event of a complicated rescue (see chapters 3 and 4). In summary, it's prudent to split four or five members into two rope teams, especially if the glacier is relatively large or in bad condition, or if the route will involve a lot of intricate weaving between crevasses.

TWO-PERSON ROPE TEAMS

Should a party of four or five divide itself into two rope teams, at least one of those teams will be a two-person team, and that pair will of course depend on just one member to hold the other's crevasse fall. In *most* cases (exceptions are discussed under "Holding the Falls") this is a reasonable chance to take, for unless a pair travels carelessly or in particularly dangerous conditions, a single climber can fairly easily resist the force generated by a crevasse fall. However, though a single climber can expect to *hold* a crevasse fall, for that single climber to *rescue* a fallen partner is another matter. Therefore, all but very experienced two-person rope teams will depend on help from another team in their party, at least to anchor the rope should one of the pair break through a snowbridge. Consequently, a party with a two-person rope team should take extra care to keep another team reasonably nearby the roped pair.

A roped pair that's part of a multiteam party can tie in about one-third of the rope's length apart, giving each member an extra third of the rope to carry coiled and securely knotted around their shoulders. On large glaciers with particularly wide crevasses—for instance, 50 to 60 feet wide in the Alaska Range and the Karakoram—the pair can increase their distance from each other, carrying less "spare" rope but ensuring that they'll be able to span the wider slots.

Two-person Parties

To team up with just one partner on a glacier excursion calls for some serious thought. While it's not unreasonable to assume that each of the pair will be able to hold the other's crevasse falls, they need to ask themselves if each can reasonably expect to then anchor the rope while holding the other's weight, and then extricate the partner. Because for many people this prospect is too demanding to be realistic, in the prudent days of yore no one ventured onto a snow-covered glacier in a party of fewer than three (or so the old-timers claim). But today the climbing community tacitly approves of two-person parties, partly because better techniques and equipment make the prospect safer, but mostly because climbers are either willing to take more risk or don't realize the greater risk they take. In particular, the push to do more technical routes, where the most efficient team size is two, has put more solitary pairs on glaciers. Most climbers, if they think about it much, want and (perhaps unknowingly) assume that they travel with the safety net of their partner anchoring them off and potentially rescuing them. However, although single-handed rescue is possible, relatively few climbers know how demanding it can be.

Assuming that two climbers are sufficiently competent, each member should tie in with enough spare rope to reach the other should he be dangling in a crevasse—tying in about 5 feet farther than one-third from an end will do the job. Thus, with a 165-foot rope, each member ties in about 60 feet (one-third of 165 feet, plus 5 feet) from an end, and carries this extra rope coiled and securely knotted over the shoulder; the pair travels with about 45 feet of rope between them. The actual footage can't be exact, of course, but it's wiser to err on the side of carrying more rope and having less rope between members, to ensure enough is available to reach each other.

On the giant glaciers of the subarctic and Karakoram, 45 feet of rope will not span many of the huge crevasses. Two-person parties going out on these glaciers should consider traveling either with a much longer rope or with two ropes. With two 165-foot ropes, each partner ties into one end of one rope, and about 75 feet from the other end of the other rope. This leaves the partners 75 feet apart, and with 90 feet of extra rope to carry.

Figure 2.1 summarizes the spans between members for rope teams of various sizes. For a team of any number, an easy way to measure off tie-in locations on the rope is to count arm spans; with arms outstretched, the distance from fingertip to fingertip is nearly the same as the measurer's height.

Crevasse falls rarely put a severe strain on a rope. It has long been accepted that approved "half ropes" of 9 millimeters (or now, even smaller diameters) are adequate for glacier travel.

Solo Glacier Travel

Some of today's alpine climbing greats climb solo, unroped. It's said that great climbers know the crevasse hazard more intimately, so they can travel safely by carefully choosing

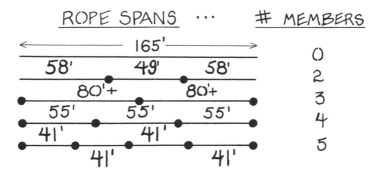

ROPE SPANS ···   # MEMBERS

Figure 2.1   Recommended rope spans between team members

when and where they go. This is true to some extent, but it's at least as true that these climbers simply are willing to take more risk. Unroped climbers generally cannot afford a single crevasse fall. While we can be impressed at the exploits of Reinhold Messner, he was able to escape a crevasse on Everest only by sheer luck; the crevasse hazard finally caught up to the great solo climber Renatto Casarotto, and it has for other experienced solo climbers.

At least two Alaskan climbers have devised techniques to make solo glacier travel safer. One was Charlie Porter, who attached a long aluminum pole to his pack. The idea was that, if he fell in, it would bridge the crevasse and he would use it to clamber out.

The other was Dave Johnston, who built a more complex arrangement called "Bridge-it." This was something like a ladder with skis on both ends; he'd walk or ski between the girders of this thing, dragging it along with the idea that, should he punch in, it would bridge the crevasse and he'd walk out on it. It also served as a sled to carry his load. I don't know if either of these arrangements were tested in crevasse falls, but one clear disadvantage is that in order to span a crevasse the bridge must be fairly perpendicular to its direction. At this time such inventions are interesting, but they can't be generally recommended.

Knots and Harnesses

A person on the end of a rope should tie in directly to his harness, using a proven knot like the figure-eight retrace. Those somewhere along the rope's span can clip a figure-eight on a bight or butterfly knot into a good locking carabiner paired with a standard carabiner, then reversing the two gates.

Glacier travelers need to pay special attention to their harness systems, because crevasse falls often leave one dangling in free space for a long time. In this situation two criteria are crucial to survival: that your harness support you as comfortably as possible (don't laugh!) with as much surface area as possible, and that it keep you from hanging upside down. To these ends you'll want a harness with especially broad webbing or fabric, and one whose waistband cinches just *above* your hipbones, supporting you with a high center of gravity (see fig. 2.2). "Swami belt" tie-ins without leg loops should never be used, for a climber dangling from one essentially hangs from the diaphragm and suffocates in minutes. Harnesses improvised from runner-webbing constrict circulation and should be avoided.

The second criterion, prevention from hanging upside down, concerns the least-appreciated trauma of falling into a crevasse. Good preparation for anyone going out on a glacier is to hang from a tree upside down in his seat harness, and feel his breathing falter and his head fill with blood until it feels ready to explode. Tree-hanging is also a good test of a seat harness's center of gravity. If you need a lot of effort from your stomach muscles to hold yourself upright, your seat harness alone is inadequate.

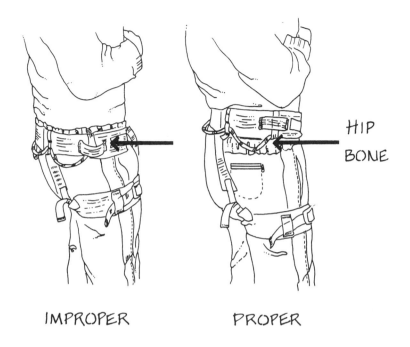

IMPROPER   PROPER

Figure 2.2   Properly and improperly fitting waist har-
                nesses

If your seat harness supports you with a high center
of gravity, if you're not wearing a pack, and if you don't
plan on being knocked unconscious in a fall, then it may
be reasonable to expect that you can fall into a crevasse
without tipping over. But if your harness doesn't really
reach over your hipbones, or if you're just naturally top-
heavy, and especially if you wear a pack much heavier than
five or ten pounds, then it's wise to use one of a few different methods to keep yourself upright.

The tried and true method is to wear a full-torso (body)
harness. Unfortunately, body harnesses have not caught

on in the U.S., because of the assumed inconvenience in adjusting clothing with one on, so it might take a special order or a trip to Canada or Europe to find one.

The American answer has been to wear a chest harness in conjunction with a seat harness. Some people are quick to point out, however, that in serious falls the two elements of this seat/chest system can compress together, bowing and potentially injuring the middle spine. In summary, a full-body harness is the safest system, a seat/chest system is nearly as safe, and a well-designed seat harness is adequate for those who don't carry much of a pack and who don't mind taking a little more risk.

For those who choose a seat/chest system, an effective chest harness can be improvised with webbing and a carabiner (see fig. 2.3). Make sure that this harness fits quite snugly, and won't ride up around your neck. In this rig see how the rope runs only through the chest harness's carabiner, holding the climber's body upright, but with his weight still bearing directly on the seat harness. *Never* knot the climbing rope into any chest harness, for then you'll hang from it; at least one glacier traveler has been strangled this way. For a similar reason, make your seat-harness tie-in knot short, to be sure it doesn't reach up to the chest harness and jam into it before bearing on the seat harness.

If you're wearing a pack, another (somewhat untested) solution is to clip the climbing rope to a sturdy strap on the pack, at or just below shoulder level, but not where the rope will press against your neck in a fall (see fig. 2.4). In effect this makes your pack work as a modestly effective chest harness, and a stiff pack may help eliminate the compression of seat/chest systems. With this in mind, pack manufacturers could build packs with extra-strong shoulder/sternum strap systems, or you can hitch a small length of webbing around one of the shoulder straps. Those roped between two partners will want to clip only one of

Figure 2.3   Improvising a chest harness

Figure 2.4   Improvising a chest harness by clipping
                   the rope to a pack strap

the two strands leading from the harness. When you do
end up in a crevasse with a pack on, this pack-clip method
also allows you to immediately jettison your pack onto the
climbing rope. If you're already using a chest harness, you
can still achieve this convenience by traveling with a runner on the pack clipped to the rope.

Yet another solution is to tie in with the kiwi coil system, which forms a modestly effective chest harness out of rope coils. (See appendix 2.)

A final concern with any of these methods that keep you upright is that when you hold a partner's crevasse fall, these methods, to varying degrees, pull you headfirst toward the falling partner. Thus far, no case history has pointed this out as a serious problem, but obviously it will be harder to resist a fall when you are pulled headlong, and if you are a solitary partner, it can be more awkward to anchor the rope once you hold the fall.

Clothing

It's tough to climb in tropical temperatures and still be ready for an instant drop into a refrigerator, but often that's what glacier travel calls for. On a sunny summer day a reflecting glacier at altitude can be incredibly hot, but of course inside the crevasses the temperature remains around freezing or colder—hypothermia is one of the principle killers of crevasse victims. Having clothing handy in the pack is important, but too often a crevasse fall leaves the victim wedged or partly buried, and the pack is inaccessible.

The best answer is to wear clothing that ventilates. "Pit-zips," knicker socks to roll down, full-zip wind pants, and synthetic insulations in general all make for a clothing system that's comfortable in a wide range of temperatures. One valuable item for sunny days is a thick shirt that's white, which will reflect the sun but will still insulate in a crevasse. Also, it's easy to keep a warm hat handy, to quickly insulate the part of your body that loses more heat than any other. Finally, perhaps the most important concern is that your hands be ready for work inside a crevasse. Either overdress them or carry gloves or mittens very handy—on your wrists or harness, or in a pocket.

Rescue Gear

The final preparation step before a team heads onto a glacier is to make sure they have adequate rescue gear. This gear should be evenly distributed among the party members and readily accessible. Use of rescue gear will be discussed in the next chapter, but it should consist of prussiks tied onto the rope ahead of each climber (if ascenders are used, have these clipped onto the seat harness, not on the rope); pulleys; runners, both long and short; anchors appropriate to the surface conditions; belay plates; and spare carabiners. Following this system, a party of three on a temperate glacier is minimally but adequately equipped for a crevasse rescue if each member clips on a pulley, a runner, an anchor and two or three spare carabiners, as well as their prussiks or ascenders. Ice axes in hand, the team is ready to embark, assuming they know where they're going.

Routefinding

Before a party gets on a glacier, they will do themselves a favor if they get the best possible overview of the glacier. From an overview they can see the overall patterns and concentrations of the glacier's crevasses and icefall and avalanche zones, and they can plan their general route accordingly. Aerial photos often provide the best overview of a glacier route, and are especially valuable in Alaska. Once you're involved in the intricacies of a route, glacier terrain can look much different than from farther away, and a party will often be tempted to alter their original plans. But unless they come across barriers or options that they obviously couldn't have seen from afar, the wisest choice is to remember the wisdom of their overview and stick with their proposed route.

Whether you can get an overview or not, the basic matter of routefinding amounts to simple geometry: the shortest way is a straight line, and if there's something in the way, you'll either have to go around it or go over it, usually the former. Keeping track of your location on a map as you go can pay off, both in case you come across features you didn't expect, and in case clouds move in and cause a whiteout.

In the winter and early spring, when snow smooths over the terrain, one can't always be sure where the simple mountain slopes end and the crevassed glacier begins. In this case, "outside" information can be the best guide, especially previous experience in the area, a good topographical map (although many glaciers have advanced or retreated dramatically since most USGS maps were compiled) or aerial photos. Also, the lower reaches of sizable glaciers are generally confined to valleys, while almost *all* slopes in the upper reaches of a glacier's basin will be glaciated, crevassed terrain. When there's doubt, treat it as crevasse country and rope up.

The Rope Leader

While overall route planning usually comes out of a team discussion, the rope leader, by virtue of his or her position at the front of the party, must discover the route's details. It's he or she who decides whether to go around crevasses or over them, when to fan out *en echelon* (described below), and whether or not a place is likely to be safe for gathering together.

Depending on the glacier and its condition, the rope leader's job can be casual or harrowing. The leader needs to start assessing the likelihood of crevasse falls before even getting on the glacier. Once traveling, the leader steadily reevaluates the strength and predictability of the snow, taking the team either over or around snowbridges. At first a wise leader will take a very conservative approach, at least until he's gathered more information along the way. If conditions are obviously solid, the leader might soon be walking and hopping across the smaller crevasses without breaking stride. If conditions are obviously hazardous, he might be poking around and weaving a course as if through a minefield.

The rope leader tries to balance two somewhat contradictory demands: safety and speed. Of course, no one wants to walk into a crevasse, but no one wants to spend a whole morning getting around one either. The rope leader decides whether a faster, more direct route (generally speaking, a route crossing a crevasse) offers enough safety compared to a longer, apparently less dangerous route (generally, a route circumventing a crevasse).

It might be easy for the safety-conscious to say, "Always take a longer, safer route," but in many cases speed *is* safety, especially when conditions will deteriorate with time—as they often do. The sun of a hot day melting snowbridges, a storm or whiteout or nightfall moving in (whether imminently or eventually), avalanche or icefall hazard from above —all these are hazards that a team can best deal with by just plain moving fast. Too, detours can exact a cost in the members' fatigue, slowing travel down even more. On the other hand, one should not risk, say, a fifty-fifty chance of taking a crevasse plunge if in any way it can be avoided, for a crevasse fall can suddenly demand all the time, energy and stress a team can spare.

When a rope leader comes across a suspected or obvious snowbridge, he can probe with an ice ax for its depth and width. Here a long ice ax with a smooth shaft can be helpful. When a probe finds a clear lack of resistance, beware! If there's no better alternative bridge or end run, crossing the fragile bridge can be safer on hands and knees, or even lying prone, to spread body weight over a greater surface area. If a crevasse's walls are obviously solid and not too far apart, it may be possible to leap over the gap, although great leaps are less commonly possible than the photographers would have us believe.

Team Travel

When a team travels roped together, how the members manage their progress affects their well-being in two important ways. First, how the rope runs at the time of a crevasse fall has a great effect on how serious the crevasse fall is. Second, the amount of consideration and teamwork each member practices can greatly affect partnerships—and, for instance, whether or not he or she will have tent space to share that night.

To minimize the seriousness of crevasse falls, the most important thing team members can do is to keep as much slack out of the rope between them as possible. Any slack in the rope is distance that a falling climber accelerates (at 32 feet per second per second!) *before* the adjacent partner can begin to brake the fall. With a slack-free rope, the force comes onto the adjacent partner immediately, before the falling climber gets very far into the hole and before the fall generates an impact velocity. Thus, with a slack-free rope most crevasse falls can be held simply by leaning against the pull, without resorting to self-arrest (see fig. 2.5).

Figure 2.5   Holding a moderate crevasse fall

Slack-free does not mean taut, however. Ideally the rope simply drapes from each climber's harness and runs to the next with neither slack nor tension (see fig. 2.6). A climber who constantly pulls rope tension on his partners generates emotional tension as well.

Glacier travel would be a simple matter of parading

Figure 2.6   Appropriate amount of slack rope

together on a snug rope if it weren't for people's different paces, and for hills and corners in the way. These factors must be coordinated. Obviously, the team can go no faster than its slowest member—faster climbers must have patience, and dawdling climbers must consider their partners! Other than this, a simple rule of thumb can greatly help rope coordination: each member tries to keep the proper amount of slack in the rope ahead.

By this rule, when one member starts up a hill and slows down, the partner behind slows down as well. When the person ahead reaches easier ground or starts downhill, the partner behind tries to speed up some, although here the person ahead must also take it a bit easier. Experienced travelers can anticipate speeding and slowing, and at appropriate times give bursts of effort to steady the overall progress, knowing that a slowing rest will shortly come.

In addition to keeping the rope free of slack, to reduce the seriousness of crevasse falls members need to concern themselves with keeping the rope perpendicular to the direction of the surrounding crevasses. When a climber falls into a crevasse and the rope is oblique to the crevasse wall, he or she will pendulum farther into the crevasse (accelerating at something less than 32 feet per second per second), coming to rest at a point directly below the adjacent partner who held the fall. With the rope nearly *paralleling* a crevasse there's also the danger that two or more members will end up over the same crevasse, and if one goes in the other(s) probably will too.

Thus, when a rope leader chooses to circumvent a crevasse, the other members heading around it should not follow the leader's tracks to the edge of the crevasse; they should start moving in the leader's direction, keeping the rope as perpendicular to the crevasse as possible. Of course, they must be careful not to walk into another crevasse.

Turning a corner, which usually means end-running a crevasse, requires similar but more subtle coordination (see fig. 2.7). As the member ahead starts around the corner, the following member still travels somewhat toward the other, and slack tends to accumulate (see figs. 2.7a and b). Thus the lead member should speed up some and the following one should slow (fig. 2.7c). When the rope span is halfway "around" the corner they reach an inflection point, and the two travel somewhat away from each other, tending to generate tension. To compensate, the lead member slows and the following one speeds up (fig. 2.7d).

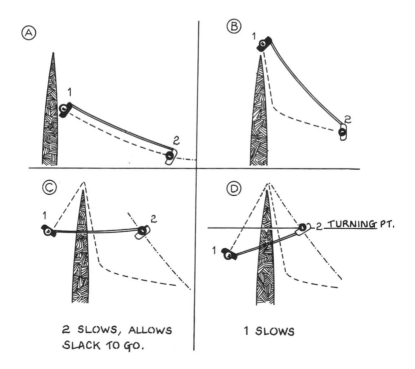

Figure 2.7   Turning a corner or end-running a crevasse *(top view)*

When crevasses run generally perpendicular to a team's intended route, keeping the rope perpendicular to them poses little problem. But when the crevasses generally parallel a party's route, the only solution is to travel *en echelon*, where members travel not in the leader's path but take their own parallel course off to the side (see fig. 2.8). While *en echelon*, ideally team members travel in the same direction but on opposite sides of the crevasses. In this case all members must coordinate their individual courses with their partners'.

However, ideal conditions for traveling *en echelon* don't often arise. Crevasse systems can lead members in different directions, making it difficult to coordinate travel or even to return together. In a heavily crevassed area one member might come to a dead end and then the whole

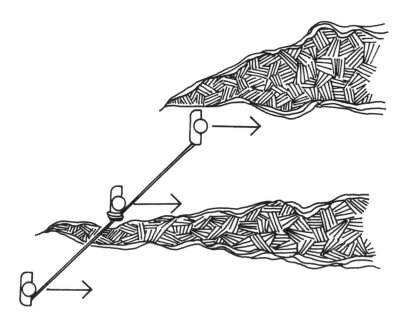

Figure 2.8   Traveling *en echelon*

team must retreat until that member can find a way around. Too, if there are novices in the party it might be wise not to trust their ability to avoid crevasses on their own. This means that, before deciding to fan out, a party must balance its potential safety with its practicality.

Whiteouts

Glaciers exist because they're in cloudy places that receive more snow than sunshine, and it's an unfortunate fact that light refracts through clouds about the same way it reflects off snow—giving clouds and snow the same white color. All too often clouds envelop a glacier, making the world white, destroying any sense of depth, diffusing even the nearest bumps and dips into a seemingly infinite, omnipotent whiteness. Disorientation in such a featureless world can be profound even in a familiar area, and it can seep into the emotional corners of the mind. In whiteouts even experienced climbers have made the most basic mistakes, for instance mistaking east for west while looking at their compasses. So the first rule about traveling in whiteouts is to avoid it.

When the first rule must be broken, the second rule is to assess the situation analytically, gathering all the information available to you. It's very helpful to have your own or someone else's tracks definitely leading where you want to go, but realize how dependent you are on those tracks. Think twice about going farther if there's a chance of snowfall or wind filling them in. Climbs or expeditions where snowfall is likely to obscure tracks will mark their routes with wands, as close as a rope's length apart if conditions could get really bad. But if you're without tracks or wands you still have a chance if you're good with a map and compass.

For a map to help, you need to establish where you are on the map, and plot a course on it to where you want

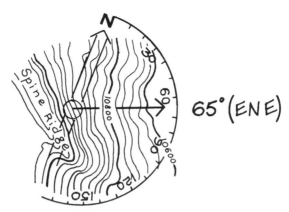

Figure 2.9   Compass bearing directly downslope will
be perpendicular to contour lines on map

to go. You'll need to locate yourself as precisely as possible, potentially with only one piece of information: the
direction of up and down. Take a compass bearing directly down your whited-out slope, and on the topographical map find the slopes on which you could possibly be
standing—that is, slopes where the contour lines run perpendicular to your reading (see fig. 2.9). Chances are there
won't be more than a couple of possible slopes. To help
you find just where you are on that slope, an altimeter can
be invaluable. Of the altimeters commonly available, only
the expensive ones are accurate enough to be really helpful, and even these should be calibrated to a mapped elevation at least once a day.

Once you've formed a hypothesis of where you are,
plot a course on the map, and take careful note of the
aspects of the slopes that your planned route should take
you across. Then set your compass to the bearing of your
plotted route and start out on that bearing. As you go,
frequently compare the aspects of the slopes you've trav-
eled (by taking bearings directly downhill again) against
those of your hypothesized plot. Based on this you can

reevaluate your hypothesis, and if the new information doesn't jibe, make a new hypothesis.

In following a compass bearing, it can help to give the compass to the person behind the lead member. This second person sights along the rope going to the leader and directs the course; the lead member has nothing to sight against, and will more easily stray from the bearing.

These procedures can work well in an area with relatively "typical" slopes, but in gentle, featureless terrain or in heavily crevassed, "densely featured" terrain there may be no solution but to wait for visibility. A friend of mine was stuck in a whiteout on the extensive plains of the Columbia Icefield. He and his partner so easily lost their way that they probably saved their lives by digging a snow cave and waiting for visibility rather than wandering in desperate hope of a way out—even though they waited for five days without food or water.

Holding the Falls: The Glacier Traveler's Belays

Usually team members depend on one another's body weight, readiness and ability to self-arrest (in that order) to hold their crevasse falls. Warnings from the leader about potentially weak bridges can emphasize to the other members the importance of a slack-free rope, since a crevasse fall coming onto a partner via a snug rope often won't pull him off his feet. If it does, then he immediately goes into self-arrest. In areas that are potentially more dangerous, it's smart to carry your ax with a self-arrest grip.

However, more hazardous crevasse crossings with longer potential falls call for a more substantial belay. There are four general cases (see fig. 2.10):

1. Crossing fragile bridges over wide crevasses;
2. Crossing fragile bridges where for one reason or another the rope runs oblique to the crevasse;

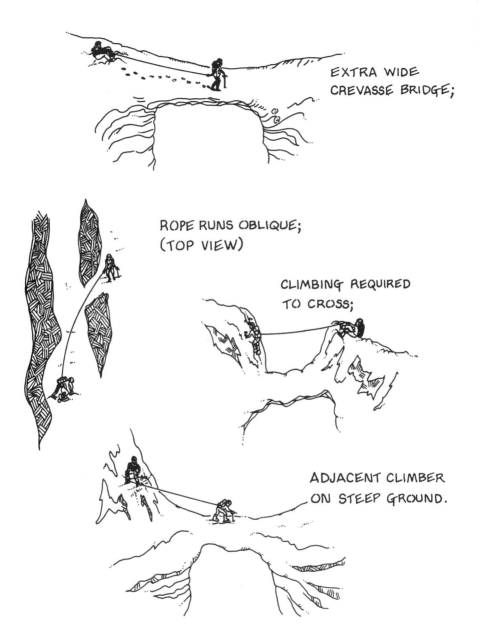

EXTRA WIDE
CREVASSE BRIDGE;

ROPE RUNS OBLIQUE;
(TOP VIEW)

CLIMBING REQUIRED
TO CROSS;

ADJACENT CLIMBER
ON STEEP GROUND.

Figure 2.10   Dangerous situations where a belay
                might be needed

3. Crevasse crossings where one must climb down the near wall and/or climb out the opposite wall; and

4. When the adjacent climber is on steep and/or icy ground above the crevasse.

Of course, it's a matter of judgment what is "wide," "oblique" or "steep." Also, in any of these situations, the severity of the force on the adjacent or belaying climber will be much greater if the crevasse lip is hard and icy.

Climbers have developed a number of methods for belaying on snow and ice, especially for holding falls of moderate potential. Of these I'll describe the boot-ax belay, for in the United States this is the most popular, yet too often it is poorly executed. For crossings with more serious fall potential, the standard anchored sitting belay should be the method of choice.

Carefully study the drawing of the boot-ax belay (figs. 2.11a to d). This is how to set it up:

1. Sink your ax nearly to the head, tilting it back from the potential force about 45 degrees. You might have to

Figure 2.11a   Boot-ax belay

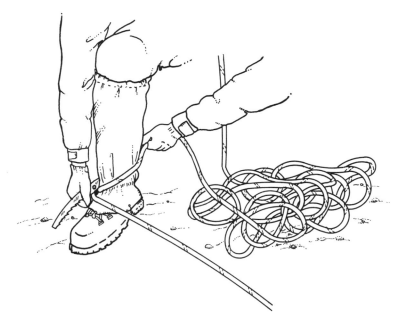

Figure 2.11b   Holding weight with boot-ax belay

stamp on it to get it into hard, late-summer snow, or in soft conditions you might have to stamp down a firmer platform.

2. Loop the rope around the shaft (fig 2.11b).

3. Press your "uphill" boot—the one away from the load—against the shaft under both strands of the rope, and take the rope in your "downhill" hand (fig. 2.11c). This is your brake hand, ready to hold a fall by wrapping the rope around your ankle, thereby bending the rope in an S-curve. Take careful note of the solid stance shown, with the climber ready to lean on the bent "uphill" leg (fig. 2.11a).

To hold a fairly hard fall with this belay, you must be practiced and ready to make it a *dynamic* belay. That is, you must dissipate the force of the fall gradually, by letting rope through for a second or two, wrapping it around your

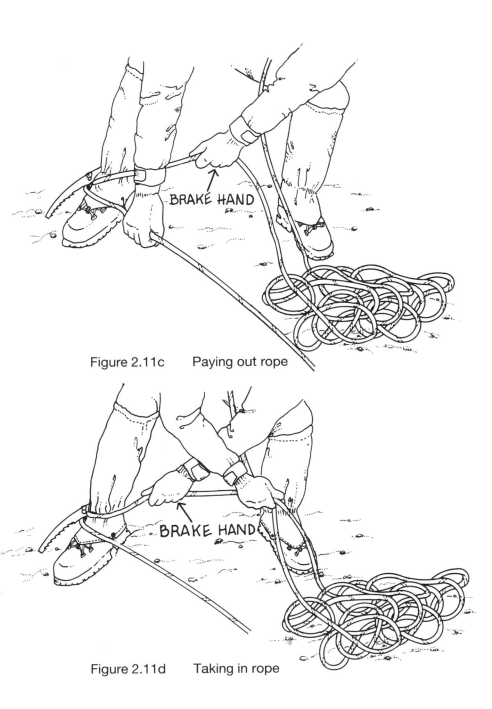

Figure 2.11c   Paying out rope

Figure 2.11d   Taking in rope

ankle gradually. The boot-ax belay cannot be expected to hold a hard fall statically, without any rope paying out— the ax and your stance will rip out.

A practiced belayer can set up a boot-ax belay literally in seconds, and with reasonably good snow and a solid, balanced stance it will hold a surprising force. However, as with any belay designed to hold only moderate falls, it is imperative to practice and develop judgment about when it can and cannot be trusted. Spend time with a partner on a steep slope of summer snow, taking in and paying out rope and holding mock falls with it.

When you're faced with the relatively unusual case of a fairly serious crevasse crossing, you'll want to set up an anchored sitting belay, just as in rock or ice climbing (see fig. 2.12). It will take more time to set an anchor and rig this belay, but with a well-placed anchor in reasonable snow it will hold the force of virtually any crevasse fall. Anchors are discussed in the rescue chapter, so here suffice it to say that you set an anchor, making sure you set it to hold in the direction that the potential fall will come from. Tie into the anchor with a runner or the climbing rope, sit down between the climber and the anchor with a mini- mum of slack in your tie-in, and rig a hip belay or belay device. Compared to a hip belay, a sticht plate or other belay device is more foolproof, and is easily rigged with a pack on. It's a good idea to carry a sticht plate for use in a rescue-hauling rig anyway, as described in the rescue chapter.

When setting up any belay across a crevasse, it's cru- cial to realize that if the climber does fall very far at all, the rope will have to be anchored off. With three or more in a party this usually isn't a problem, as a free member should be able to come over to the belay and do the job. But a two-person party must take this fact more seriously, as the belayer will have to anchor the rope alone, while holding the weight of the fallen partner. It takes a lot of skill and nerve to do this while holding a boot-ax belay, and it's no

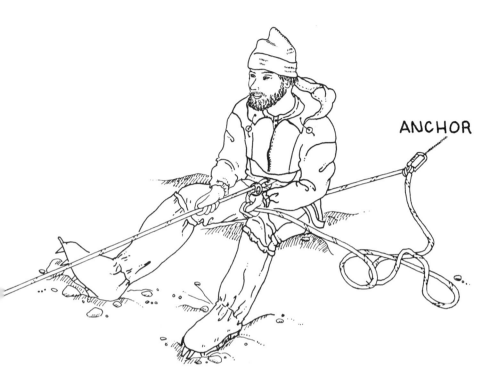

ANCHOR

Figure 2.12   Anchored sitting belay

mean feat while holding a hip belay. Therefore, two-person parties needing more than self-arrest as a belay should depend on an anchored sitting belay, with a belay device.

Gathering Together

Most rest stops can be taken with the members still stretched apart along their rope, but when a team does gather together and slacken the rope, the lead member and the party as a whole must carefully choose the spot. To make sure the area hides no crevasses, the leader should probe it with the rope still stretched out. Then the last member into the site should be brought in with a boot-ax belay, and the established "safe zone" should be made known to all members, perhaps with wands. When leaving the spot the rope leader should then receive a belay. Any time a party stays in one place, they of course should be especially careful to be-out of the way of icefall, rockfall or avalanche runout.

Travel on a "Dry" Ablation Zone

Where no snow covers a glacier's skeleton of ice, travel precautions are much different. Here there are no snow-bridges to break through, and all the crevasses are apparent. But to simply travel roped up as on a snowy surface is to court disaster; on the ice members cannot hold falls, and a rope merely would assure that one's fall would include the rest. Hence members travel as they would on similar terrain on rock or general alpine terrain—unroped, unless the climbing is steep and/or exposed enough to require an anchored belay.

Camping Considerations

Disposal of human waste is a serious concern on a glacier, and there is no ideal sewage disposal. The first choice is to defecate off the glacier, in soil or moraine where contamination of water is minimized. If you must go on the glacier, get the waste into a deep crevasse. Usually in camp this means you dig a potty and line it with a bag stretched out between wands, for transport later to a crevasse. Bags should be either biodegradable plastic or (in fair weather) paper grocery sacks, doubled in either case.

Another possibility on a temperate glacier in the summer is to camp near a crevasse with a solid edge, making this a direct latrine. Set an anchor and fix a rope to the edge, making sure that there's no overhanging lip (or else clearing a small lip away), and with a swami tie-in and prussik self-belay members can lean back and—well, unload. Direct crevasse latrines are certainly preferred while on the go, and for this reason it's better to have a harness with leg loops that drop away, or else you'll have to rig a separate waist belt.

Camping near a solid crevasse also allows sound disposal of urine and food waste. If a solid-edged crevasse is not available, a urination site should be designated and the waste concentrated. Remember, on a glacier the water source is the snow.

So far we can only speculate if crevasse-buried waste does or does not contaminate glacial meltwater; certainly much depends on the type of glacier and the distance from the terminus. But crevasse burial is certainly better than surface burial, which melts out. Mt. Rainier National Park now requires climbers to either backpack the waste out or use one of their outhouses, where waste is flown out.

A couple of final aesthetic courtesies: camp at least a short distance off a well-traveled trail, so other climbers don't have to walk through your campsite; and retrieve and pack out any wands you've placed.

CHAPTER 3

RESCUE TECHNIQUES FOR THE GLACIER TRAVELER

The previous chapter discussed the precautions that glacier travelers can take to guard against crevasse falls. But being prepared and careful doesn't change the fact that a part of traveling on glaciers is occasionally falling into crevasses. Therefore, knowing both how to ascend out of a crevasse and how to haul a partner out of one have long been accepted as essential skills for the glacier traveler. This chapter outlines the fundamentals of these skills, and the following chapter adds more advanced techniques to make crevasse rescue reliable in more situations.

Ascending Systems

Most crevasses that people fall into trap their victims between unclimbable walls of soft snow overhung by looser snow, so to get out of a typical crevasse a person needs a system for ascending the rope. Big-wall climbers, spelunkers and glacier travelers all have developed various systems for ascending a rope. Each system uses a set of two or more rope-gripping devices, either mechanical ascenders or prussik (or similar) knots. With all your weight on one ascender or knot, the other, unweighted one is free to be moved up the rope; then you shift all your weight to the "new" one and raise the other, repeating the process up the rope. As well as using various knots or camming devices, systems differ in how they connect which body parts to the knots or ascenders.

Though mechanical ascenders are somewhat faster and easier to use than knots, few glacier travelers feel that an occasional crevasse rescue justifies their added weight and expense. Unless a party carries ascenders for a technical climb anyway, most people find that a good prussik system works fine. Also, prussiks are safer because they generally grip better on icy ropes, and under a shock load an ascender can either destroy the rope or can break more easily than a prussik.

A prussik knot is made from a loop of supple rope, usually 6-millimeter perlon. The best knot to tie the loop is a grapevine or "double fisherman's" knot. To make a prussik knot from the loop you simply wrap it through itself two or three times around a rope of larger diameter (see fig. 3.1). Essentially, then, the prussik knot is a double or triple girth hitch. Straighten the wraps so that they coil cleanly and snugly around the main rope. Then, when you pull on the open loop the wraps grab; the more you pull the more tightly they grab, because the wraps are snugging onto themselves. But when you loosen the wraps

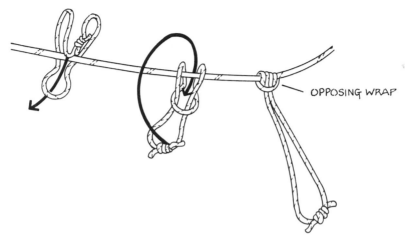

Figure 3.1   Tying a prussik knot

and hold them directly, they slide freely along the main rope. After a person's body weight has wrenched the wraps tightly, an easy way to loosen them is to press against the single "opposing" wrap designated in the drawing.

A prussik's friction relies on the suppleness and smaller diameter of the prussik cord. With climbing ropes of either 9 or 11 millimeters in diameter, the best compromise between strength and bite is a 6-millimeter prussik. However, a somewhat stiff 6-millimeter prussik on a somewhat stiff 9-millimeter rope will definitely need that third wrap to keep it from slipping. When new, a single strand of 6-millimeter perlon will hold up to 1,700 pounds, but it should nevertheless be replaced frequently. Some climbers favor marine braid Dacron cord for their prussiks because its very supple sheath grabs extremely well. However, be aware that this softer sheath wears faster than the stiffer but tougher perlon. The new 5.5-millimeter Spectra cord seems to be a suitable ultra-strong prussik material. Kevlar cord should never be used for a prussik because it's quite stiff and its fibers readily break down with repeated flexing.

Of all the connecting systems, the "Texas" system has drawn the most favor among glacier travelers for its simplicity, lightness, comfort and ease of use. It consists of a simple prussik loop (made from 35 to 40 inches of cord) clipped to a locking or doubled carabiner on the seat harness, and another prussik knot with a pair of extensions and small loops for the feet (see fig. 3.2).

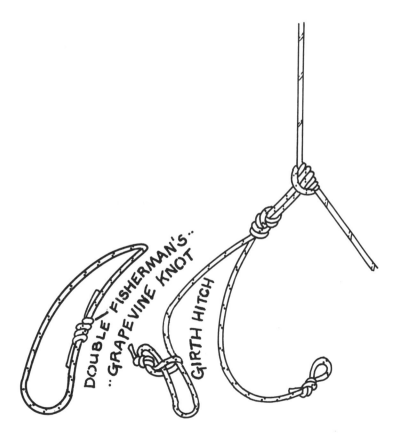

Figure 3.2   Texas prussik system

The foot loops, or "stirrups," are best constructed from a single strand 7 to 8 feet long, as follows:

1. In the middle of this strand tie a figure eight with a bight at least 6 inches long.

2. Stand and hold this bight at your diaphragm, so the two strands drape down to the ground.

3. At the point where each strand reaches the ground, tie an overhand knot that leaves a bight of about 3 inches. Trim off any extra cord.

To make these overhand knots into a cinching loop for a boot of any size, with or without crampons, you simply feed the main cord through the loop as a girth hitch.

When roping up for glacier travel, wrap both the waist and stirrup prussiks on the rope between you and a partner, the stirrups adjacent to your harness, the waist loop next to them. Clip the waist prussik to a locking carabiner on the harness, and either tuck the stirrups away in a pocket, or knot and clip them off on the harness. If you're using mechanical ascenders, keep them handy on the harness, *not* on the rope, because in a crevasse fall the weighty objects spring up at about face level and typically knock the victim silly. Most models can readily be put on the rope when needed.

Here's a summary of how to ascend with the Texas system (see fig. 3.3a to c):

1. Girth-hitch your feet into the stirrups, then stand tall in them. To keep strain off your arms while standing up, bring your feet under your buttocks and press up using your thighs (fig. 3.3a).

2. As you rise, loosen the waist prussik and slide it up the rope with you (fig. 3.3b).

3. Sit back on the waist prussik, and lift your feet as high as possible (fig. 3.3c).

4. With the weight now off the stirrups, slide them up as high as possible, even to where they meet the waist prussik.

Figure 3.3a   Ascending with the Texas prussik system using leg muscles: bring feet underneath buttocks, then stand.

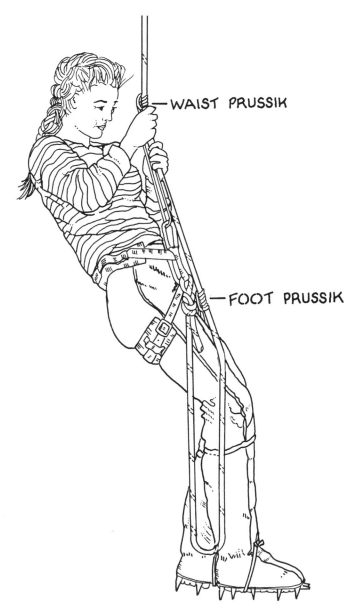

—WAIST PRUSSIK

—FOOT PRUSSIK

Figure 3.3b   Stand tall, bringing waist prussik up as you rise

PACK

Figure 3.3c   Resting from the waist prussik, slide the
foot prussik as high as possible.

5. Kick your feet under your buttocks to stand tall and repeat the process.

The Texas system keeps your weight balanced by having you straddle the rope, and you spend over half your ascent time hanging relatively comfortably in your seat harness. Chest harnesses interfere with raising the waist prussik in this system, so they should be unclipped while ascending.

In any ascending system the only safety is the prussik or ascender that connects to your waist harness. As reliable as most systems are, if you're ascending more than just 15 or 20 feet it's wise to back it up by clipping a bighted figure eight from the main rope right below the lower prussik or ascender into another locking carabiner on your harness.

Whatever ascending system you use, however, it's important to practice using it before it's needed; throwing a rope over a tree limb can make for at least a rudimentary practice session.

Prussik or Ascender as Self-belay

A prussik or ascender can also be used to belay oneself along a rope on a glacier's surface. The prussik or ascender connects from an anchored and taut rope to your seat harness. With most ascenders you should clip a carabiner from the bottom of the ascender across the rope; this keeps the ascender in line with the rope, because when you fall at 90 degrees to the anchor's axis an ascender tends to wrench off the rope. With the prussik or ascender set up, you're free to move along the rope in either direction, sliding the prussik or ascender as you go. Should a snowbridge fail, you must let go of the prussik or ascender and let it hold your fall. As for ascending, it doesn't hurt to back this up with a figure-eight knot clipped into your harness as well. Self-belays come in handy during crevasse rescues; the situations when you're likely to need one are described later.

Victim Procedures

One moment you're walking on top of the glacier, the next you're falling, wrenching in a chaos of snow and darkness that seems to be pitching you into the bowels of the earth. Then, *boing!* You're jerked to a swinging, sputtering halt, and you look down between cold blue walls into an apparently infinite, dripping blackness.

Your heart races and you strain against a weight still pulling you toward the depths. Oh yes, you now recall, the first thing to do after falling in a crevasse is to get your pack off your back, and clip it onto the rope. If you were traveling with the pack already clipped to the rope, you can just heave it off. Eventually you'll want to have it clipped to the rope below your prussiks or ascenders, but for now just get it onto the rope. You can also clip off your ice ax. You may be warm with adrenaline now, but the wet darkness of a crevasse will soon chill you, so next put on some more clothes, especially to keep your hands warm.

Now look around. Is it at all reasonable to walk, climb or chimney out of the crevasse? Soon one of your buddies will be peering down at you, and a belay or lowering can be arranged. If, however, you can't climb out, and if you actually are dangling in space with your full weight on the rope, there's no reason not to simply start ascending it. True, you don't know what kind of anchor your partners may be fumbling to set up, but with your weight already fully on the rope, unless your ascending system fails there's nothing that ascending can do that they'll even notice. However, if even part of your weight is not on the rope—for example, if you're on a ledge or pressing between crevasse walls—don't surprise your partners with any additional load. In this case wait for one to peer over and assure you that the rope is well anchored.

Before you start up, clip your pack to the rope below your prussiks or ascenders. This way, as you ascend, the pack's weight will actually help you raise your lower prussik or ascender by keeping tension on the rope, and as you climb the pack will be following you on a two-to-one "pulley." You may have to keep the pack from snagging on small overhangs as you ascend. However, a heavy pack clipped like this will make it difficult or impossible to tie backup knots to your harness, so if the pack is big and your climb out is a long one, have a rope sent down to haul it up.

As you approach the lip you'll probably find that the rope disappears into overhanging snow some frustratingly short and desperately steep distance below your goal, the surface. You can shove your prussiks up into the overhang, but to get over the top you'll have to employ any of a few different tricks.

First, you may be able to scoop away much of the overhang with your ax—carefully, though, with upward-directed pushes, for a sharp ice ax can cut a weighted climbing rope as if it were cutting string. Next you'll want to get your prussiks absolutely as far up the rope as possible. Then maybe your buddies can set a prussik above the lip and from it drop down a ladder of runners for you to haul up on. Or you might get enough height if you tie a figure-eight loop in the climbing rope for one foot to stand in; tie this as high as possible right below the lower prussik. With a partner reaching for you with an outstretched ice ax, it usually doesn't take but a couple of all-out heaves to get you onto the surface.

Surface Member Procedures

As mentioned in the introduction, extracting someone from a crevasse can be a fairly technical operation. Before getting into the surface members' procedures, it's important to understand two of its elements: anchors on a glacier, and the basis of pulley hauling systems.

ANCHORS

As we've said, most crevasse falls occur where a glacier is covered with some sort of soft snow; this is the highly varying medium that glacier travelers usually depend on for anchors.

The ubiquitous anchor for snow is the deadman, or fluke, a simple metal plate with attachment cables. It works on the principle that a broad surface buried in the snow will resist a force because to move it you'll have to move all the snow in front of it. Two simple features on a snow fluke increase its reliability manyfold. First, a fluke vertically bent so the convex side faces the load will accommodate pulls slightly oblique to the fluke's plane. Second, a fluke's cables should be swaged with the upper cable longer than the lower, so that a simultaneous pull on the two cables leaves the fluke tilted back at 30 to 40 degrees from perpendicular to the pull. With this cant a fluke resists any pressure to rise out of the snow. Set properly, a fluke with these features will actually move through the snow like an airfoil when loaded, deflecting itself down and burying itself deeper. A loop of cord attached to a fluke can make it easier to retrieve once buried (see fig. 3.4).

To place a fluke well, you must first evaluate the snow. In typical old "summer" snow, you can simply dig the necessary trench (as outlined below), but in particularly slushy snow or in never-melted "new" snow you'll first need to prepare the placement area.

When the snow is quite slushy, you usually just need to scrape away and dig down to the inevitable firmer snow below. But in "new," relatively low-density snow, you'll need to simulate age-hardening. Essentially this means you dig, overturn and generally upset the snow, then stomp and repack the area. Then, before you dig in to set the fluke, wait five minutes for the broken crystals to rebond into a denser, firmer medium.

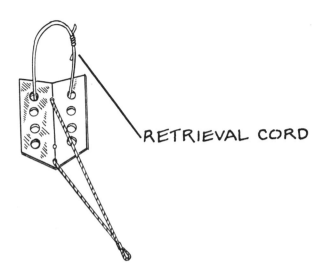

RETRIEVAL CORD

Figure 3.4   Snow fluke

One must also be wary of placing flukes if there's an icy layer not far under the surface, for such a layer can deflect a fluke upward. The layer can be either an old melt-freeze layer of some sort, or the ice surface of the glacier itself, but in either case you should use another of the anchors discussed below.

With the snow ready, you now set your fluke:

1. With the adz of your ax, dig a 1-foot-long trench perpendicular to the load and about a foot deep. Angle this trench about 30 to 40 degrees from perpendicular to the snow surface, the angle of the fluke to its upper cable.

2. With the pick of your ax, slice out a slot from the middle of the trench running toward the load. This slot is for the fluke's cables, and should be as deep as the original trench. This completes a T-shaped site.

3. Stretching out the cables toward the load, set the fluke into the trench with the upper cable parallel to the

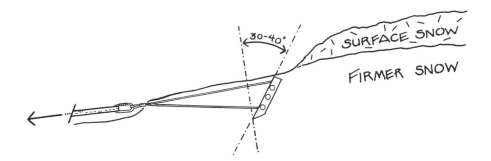

Figure 3.5   Properly placed fluke

snow surface. Set the fluke into the trench with a combination of pressing down on the fluke and pulling out on the cables.

4. Jerk the cable a couple of times and watch how the fluke reacts. If the fluke rides up when tugged, the cable slot is probably not deep enough, so it's putting a bend in the lower cable that lifts the fluke. Or, if with the tugs the fluke flaps against the trench wall rather than setting deeper, then the trench wall is not canted back enough, or you might have found an icy layer below. If the tugs set the fluke deeper, then you're in business. In any case, the crustier the snow the more critical it is to set the fluke and its cables at the correct angle. With practice, placing a fluke takes but half a minute or less (see fig. 3.5).

The other well-known snow anchor is the picket, a simple post about $2\frac{1}{2}$ feet long. Pickets are normally reserved for firmer snow. Other than having a pointed tip for driving into very hard snow and an anchor hole at the top, there are few design considerations in a picket other than surface area.

Pickets are simply driven into the snow, tilted back about 30 degrees from perpendicular to the load. Either hammer blows or boot stamps can pound one into hard snow. In very firm to very hard snow, such as old frozen snow or stiff wind-blown snow, typical on the higher reaches of mountains, pickets can be the anchor of choice. However, down on the glaciers, even in firm conditions, it's almost always more likely that a picket will lever out than that a well-placed fluke will fly out.

But there is a way to place a very reliable picket—burying it sideways, as a deadman (see fig. 3.6). As for a fluke, the procedure goes:

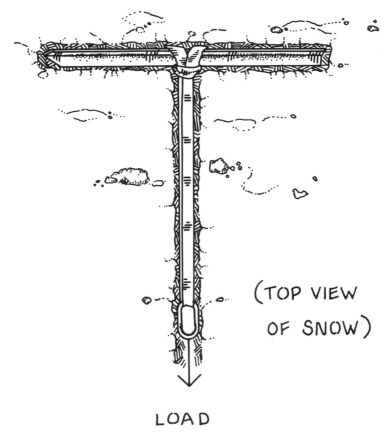

(TOP VIEW OF SNOW)

LOAD

Figure 3.6   Picket-deadman anchor *(top view)*

1. Prepare the snow if necessary, and then dig a trench as long as the picket, about a foot deep and perpendicular to the load. As you dig, undercut the trench toward the load.
2. From the center of the trench dig a trench as deep as the main one but perpendicular to it, toward the load. If this trench is not as deep as the original, there will be an upward pull on the picket.
3. Girth-hitch a runner around the center of the picket, and then stamp the picket into the trench, with the runner lying in the "T" trench. Finally, bury and stamp on everything except the tail of the runner, and you have, in most snow conditions, a very strong anchor. You can strengthen it further by plunging an ice ax or two immediately in front of it. Like any snow or ice anchor, this anchor is directional, only resisting a force perpendicular to the picket. An ice ax with a strong metal or composite shaft works equally well.

ANCHORS IN POOR SNOW CONDITIONS

In extreme conditions, when the snow is deeply slushy (like low-elevation Alaska in June), or particularly dry (like the Canadian Rockies in the fall and winter), it may be simply impossible to set a reliable fluke or picket. One anchor that might work is a couple of plunged ice axes equalized (see below) with people leaning on them. Remember, though, that the general theory of snow anchors is to resist a force with surface area. So when the snow is unconsolidated and weak, increase the surface area. For this reason improvised "deadmen" can make for the strongest anchors— for example, a pack, a pair of skis (ski poles are not strong enough), stuff sacks tightly filled with snow, or a shovel. These can be girth-hitched and thoroughly buried to give the best possible anchor in bad conditions.

ICE SCREWS

When a thin layer of snow covers the icy ablation zone of a glacier, then any crevasse fall will have to be anchored in the ice. The quickest anchor in ice is an ice screw, and in fact an ice screw in solid blue ice is more reliable than any snow anchor. Any of the tubular ice screws available work well in glacier ice, although longer models are much preferred for added strength in the often porous, softer ice of a glacier.

Just as snow anchors depend on snow quality, the most important aspect of a reliable ice screw is the quality of the ice. Glacier ice is wonderfully consistent and not brittle, but usually there's a surficial layer that you'll want to scrape away to get at the solid stuff underneath.

The most critical aspect to placing an ice screw is that it be tilted back away from the load. For the relatively moderate but prolonged loads of a rescue, it's wise to tilt a screw back a bit more than for ice climbing; 30 to 40 degrees from perpendicular to the load is the best here. However, the eye of the screw should rest flush against the ice. Here's how to place an ice screw and accommodate both these criteria:

1. Chop a small ledge into the ice at the proper angle for the eye to rest against. By canting the pick of your ice ax away from the load at the same angle the screw will be set in, with the adz you can then chop exactly the ledge you need in just a few seconds. Often you can just use or enhance a small depression in the ice.

2. Place the screw so that the tip of the eye comes to rest as nearly as possible at the edge of the ledge, pointing toward the load.

3. When the screw is loaded, the carabiner you clip into the screw should then pull at the desired 30 to 40 degrees from perpendicular to the screw's axis (see fig. 3.7). It's important to realize that pressure can cause ice to melt,

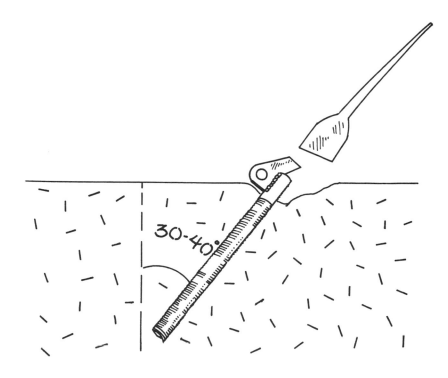

Figure 3.7   Ice screw properly set for rescue anchor
(Note: ice ax head is at proper angle to
chop ledge so that eye rests flush)

even though the ice temperature remains at or slightly below the freezing point. Thus, during the prolonged loading of a rescue, ice screws can loosen dangerously. For this reason, when rescuing on a summer day with ice-screw anchors it's wise to have a backup anchor, as described below. On very warm days ice screws can slowly loosen even without being loaded, and to alleviate this you can cover a screw with snow or ice chips and channel away any meltwater running over it.

BOLLARDS

A more tedious but very strong ice anchor is the bollard, a teardrop-shaped mushroom chopped out of the ice and looped with rope or webbing. Depending on the density of the ice, a mushroom 2 to 3 feet wide will be plenty strong; in fact, the main risk with a bollard is not the mushroom shearing off, but the rope or webbing rolling off. Therefore, it's the shape of a bollard that makes it safe or unsafe. Make sure that the load pulls downward at least slightly, and that the three sides of the mushroom that will bear the weight are well undercut.

To make a bollard:

1. Look for a relatively high spot where the load will naturally pull downward, then scrape away any surficial snow or ice that won't hold well.

2. Start by chopping the teardrop outline, gradually concentrating more on the three sides that will bear weight. Tubular adzes work best for this.

3. As your groove gets deep, small blows with the ax's pick can fine-tune the undercut lip. Before trusting a bollard with someone's weight, loop the rope or webbing over it and see what protrusions, if any, might lift it off, and eliminate them. A trustworthy bollard distributes the load around a fairly even curve, without the anchor rope running over any high spots (see fig. 3.8).

Even with practice it takes 10 to 20 minutes to chop a good bollard. Though a good one can be stronger than any ice screw and will not melt significantly, because of the time involved most people consider them as a backup to ice screws, or for cases when the need for ice anchors isn't anticipated and screws aren't carried. One can also make a surprisingly strong bollard out of firn, although here the mushroom should be at least 6 feet wide and nearly a foot deep.

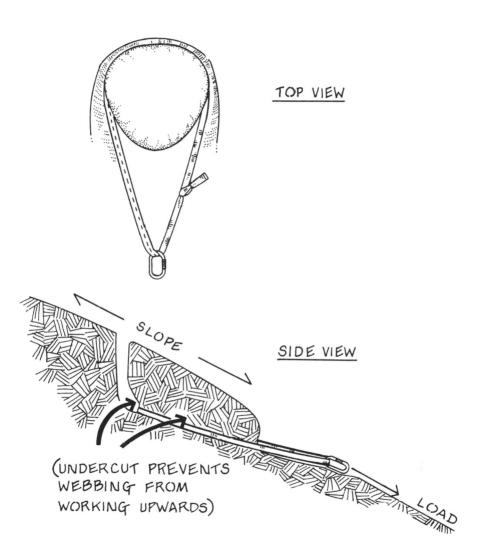

TOP VIEW

SIDE VIEW

SLOPE

(UNDERCUT PREVENTS
WEBBING FROM
WORKING UPWARDS)

LOAD

Figure 3.8   Bollard

EQUALIZING AND BACKING UP ANCHORS

Other than a magnificent bollard, no anchor in ice or snow should be singly trusted for a rescue. In coupling anchors there are three principal methods, and which to use depends on the anchor medium and the gear available.

BACKING UP. This method involves simply connecting a second anchor to the carabiner of the first one. The connection should have essentially no slack, so that if the first anchor fails the weight transfers to the second anchor immediately, without generating a shock load.

1. Measure the exact place to set the second anchor by stretching out a runner from the first anchor's carabiner, behind the first anchor.

2. Set the second anchor so that its carabiner reaches just to the end of the new runner (see fig. 3.9a).

This simple system is fine for linking two flukes, because it's normal for the primary fluke to slip a bit once it's loaded, and start sharing the load with the backup.

TENSIONED BACKUP. When a primary anchor is already loaded, you can connect the backup with tension, so that it shares the load. Do not use this until you are familiar with the tie-off.

1. Set a backup anchor "behind" the first.

2. Run webbing or climbing cord from the carabiner of the backup through a new carabiner on the primary, and back toward the backup (see fig. 3.9b).

3. Pull hard on this runner, creating tension between the backup and the load on the primary. Then clip it into the backup's carabiner.

4. Maintaining the tension, tie off the runner with a "slip hitch" tie-off, the same as for tying off a belay.

This is an excellent method to reinforce an anchor for hauling, and for linking one equalized pair with a second equalized pair–see page 91.

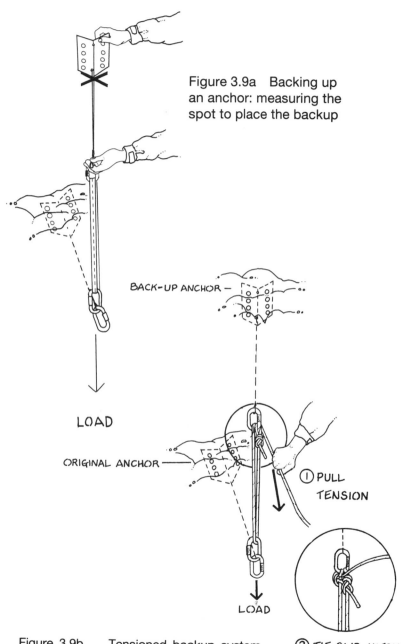

Figure 3.9a   Backing up an anchor: measuring the spot to place the backup

BACK-UP ANCHOR

LOAD

ORIGINAL ANCHOR

① PULL TENSION

LOAD

Figure 3.9b   Tensioned backup system

② TIE SLIP-HITCH

EQUALIZING. Distributing a load between a pair of anchors virtually doubles the reliability of the overall anchor. Two methods are presented here, the first quicker and more widely known, the second safer but more involved.

For the first method:

1. Clip a long runner into both anchors, and make a twist in one of the two strands between them.

2. Clip a third (locking or doubled) carabiner through this twist and across the other strand (see fig. 3.10). When this third carabiner is loaded, the two anchors share the weight between them, even from a range of directions. Should one of the anchors fail the twist will preserve the

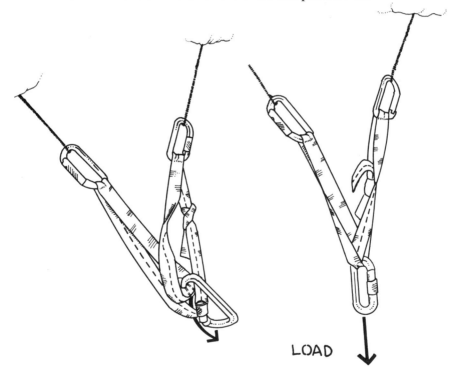

Figure 3.10   Equalizing anchors: method one

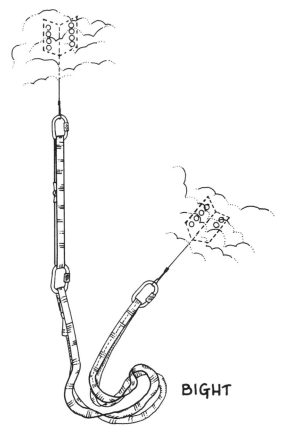

BIGHT

Figure 3.11a   Equalizing anchors: method two; clip
                    runners into two anchors.

connection to the other, but the load will come onto the
other after some movement, as a potentially severe shock
load.

For the second:

1. Clip one runner onto the rear anchor, as a simple
extension (see figs. 3.11a and b).

2. Clip a long runner into the front anchor and the
extension.

3. Pull both strands of the long runner toward the

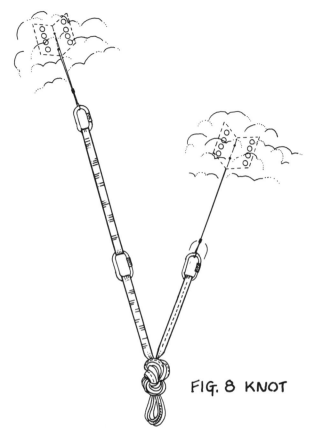

FIG. 8 KNOT

Figure 3.11b   Equalizing anchors: method two; tie an
overhand or figure-eight knot on a
bight.

projected load, and tie an overhand or figure-eight knot
on a bight. As in the first method, when a load comes
onto this bight the two anchors share the force equally.
This method uses more webbing and is slightly trickier to
tie than the first one, and the figure-eight or (especially)
overhand knot can become permanently tight after a rescue load. What makes this method safer is that, should
one of the anchors fail, that share of the load comes onto
the other anchor immediately, preventing shock loading.

In either coupling arrangement, the connecting runner should be long enough to keep the angle between the anchors smaller than 90 degrees. If a short runner connects widely spread anchors, this angle broadens, and a sort of leverage geometrically increases the force on the anchors (fig. 3.12). If a runner were tightly stretched between the anchor pair (at 180 degrees from the load), the force theoretically becomes infinite! For this reason ice screws and upright pickets should be paired nearly in line with one another, although some spread is recommended for flukes or other deadmen.

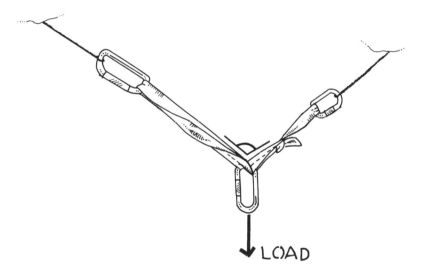

↓ LOAD

Figure 3.12   Improperly equalized anchors: broad angle multiplies force on anchor.

THE ULTIMATE, PREFERRED ANCHOR SYSTEM

The most secure anchor system backs up one equalized anchor pair with another, using four anchors in all. This arrangement is especially recommended for hauling victims using snow anchors. After setting a primary anchor pair, you use one of the backup methods described above—preferably the tensioned backup—to connect the equalizing carabiner of a second pair to the equalizing carabiner of the first.

Because ice and especially snow are such variable mediums, there's no hard and fast rule about how many anchors are enough to rescue with. In general, trust your intuition: if you're not sure, add more anchors!

THE BASICS OF PULLEY SYSTEMS

It takes a lot of force to haul someone out of a crevasse. Friction of the rope running over the crevasse lip increases the resistance, so that hauling even a partner with no pack generally takes two to five times as much force as a strong climber can generate. Therefore, all but the largest parties have to increase their hauling force by using a pulley system. In a manner analogous to low gears that enable a bicyclist to climb a hill, pulley systems distribute a load and allow even a single person to haul another out of a crevasse.

The basic "block-and-tackle" pulley system is shown in figure 3.13; the rope is anchored at a, and runs through a pulley, b, which is connected directly to the load. When the end of the rope, c, is pulled, the pulley (and thereby the load as well) moves only half as far as the rope end c. This means that the work is halved also, and the pulley and load receive twice the original force. Another way to look at it is that by looping through the pulley back to the anchor, a second force is generated, because the length of rope a-b (between the anchor and the pulley) effectively pulls on the load too.

This simple system is known as the C-pulley system, for the single curve in the rope. Theoretically it gives a 2 to 1 mechanical advantage, although with even a good rescue pulley that dissipates only 10 percent to friction, the

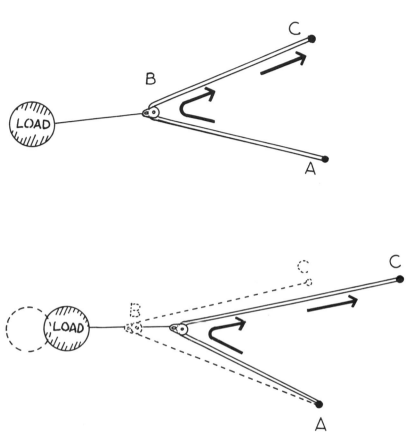

Figure 3.13   Basic pulley system

actual multiplying force will be 1.8 to 1. Also, the maximum efficiency comes only when the pulling force at c is in line with the pulley and the anchor—that is, when lines a-b and b-c are very close together. For clarity figure 3.13 has been drawn with the rope coming out from the pulley to point c at an angle, but if the force is applied to the side like this, essentially pulling partly away from the system, the force applied at c is less than doubled.

Crevasse Rescue Procedures

The general procedures for rescuing a partner from a crevasse are as follows:

1. Stop the fall.

2. Anchor the rope, leaving enough slack to reach the victim.

3. Check the victim, and decide on a rescue method. Generally speaking, the first choice is to have the victim ascend out, as previously described, and the second choice is to haul him out.

4. Prepare the crevasse lip.

5. Either assist the victim as he ascends over the lip, or set up a hauling system.

6. Haul the victim out, if necessary.

With this sequence in mind, we can detail the elements of crevasse rescue.

HOLDING A FALL

Let's return to the well-prepared three-person rope team traveling together on a glacier. Poof! One of the members disappears. The adjacent partner must hold the fall.

As stated before, if the rope is tight and fairly perpendicular to the crevasse, most snowbridge collapses can be held simply by standing firm, leaning against the pull from the fallen partner. If the rope does not come taut immediately—that is, if the victim is stopped by the snowbridge or narrow walls before his weight comes onto the partner—the partner should retreat from the crevasse and pull the rope taut. If the force of the fall pulls the adjacent member off his feet, then he must work into the self-arrest position, as should the next member down the rope. As discussed in chapter 2, the nightmare of being pulled toward an abyss, digging and kicking for every ounce of self-arrest grip, is rare, but it can happen.

Crevasse falls generally end in a split second. In minor "punch-ins" where the victim still has half his body on the surface, then "rescue" is easy. Partners on the surface stand firm with the rope tight, and with this help the victim can probably just struggle out. If the victim is in too far to heave out right away, or if he is stuck, then the surface members should anchor the rope, the first step in a "genuine" rescue.

ANCHORING THE ROPE

Besides keeping the victim from falling any farther, anchoring the rope allows surface members to be belayed out to the crevasse to assist or check the victim; it enables the victim to ascend out on the rope, if possible; and it allows the surface members to set up a hauling system.

The first and third criteria make it important to anchor the rope not at its end, but in the rope's midsection, leaving enough slack to reach the victim. This is where the proper spacing of members, as discussed in chapter 2, becomes critical. Assuming a three-person rope team has an end member fall, here's the procedure for anchoring the rope:

1. The middle member holds the rope taut, either in self-arrest or by leaning against the pull.

2. The free member on the end of the rope comes down to "below" the middleman, coming down the rope with a self-belay.

3. A reasonable distance below the middle person (but not close to the crevasse), the free person sets an equalized anchor pair. Preferably this is at least 10 to 15 feet below the middle person, to leave plenty of free rope above the anchor to reach the victim.

4. The free person then loops a three-wrap prussik (or sets an ascender) onto the taut rope leading to the victim, and clips this into the anchor. He then slides this anchoring prussik down the rope until it's fully stretched against the anchor.

5. Now the middle person cautiously moves to-

ward the crevasse, letting the victim's weight go onto the anchor. With the victim solidly anchored, both members are free to untie from the rope.

The next step is to assess his condition and position, for these things will determine the nature of the rescue. The victim and the surface members might be able to shout back and forth, but if the victim is any distance down, a surface member will have to go to the crevasse edge to establish communication.

CHECKING THE VICTIM

It should go without saying that anyone venturing near a crevasse into which someone has just fallen needs a belay. More than one would-be rescuer has unwittingly fallen to his own death. Surface members can use another rope or the slack rope "above" the anchor to belay the person going out to check the victim. One surface member can tie off to the anchor and belay another, or a solitary rescuer can go to the lip on a self-belay. If but one rope is available, using a self-belay allows the free end to be sent into the crevasse, either to haul the victim's pack, or to rappel on. While approaching the lip, however, it doesn't hurt to back up the self-belay with a figure-eight knot clipped into the harness from slightly farther down the rope. The member going out can also carry one or preferably two ice axes, and extra prussiks and runners.

Whatever the belay, it's wise to approach the crevasse lip some distance to the side of where the rope disappears, to avoid getting on the unstable lip directly above the victim and breaking it onto him. As the surface member approaches the edge, getting down on hands and knees will put less stress on the unstable lip. Then the member can either set the self-belay or instruct the belayer to hold firm while he leans out to talk with the victim and assess the situation.

Ideally, the victim is unharmed and is either preparing to ascend the rope or is already doing so. If the victim needs his pack hauled, the free end of the rope can be sent down for this. The person at the lip should wait there to assist the victim over that last desperate overhang. One way to help is to set a prussik or ascender above the lip and from this lower a ladder of runners for the victim to climb up. Another is simply to reach down with an ice ax for the victim to grab and heave up on.

If, because of injury, partial burial, or wedging or any other reason, a victim cannot ascend out, then the surface members must haul their partner out. In this case getting the victim past the overhanging remnants of the failed snowbridge can be the hardest part of the task. Preparing for this problem deserves a discussion of its own.

PREPARING CREVASSE LIPS

During a crevasse fall the rope often cuts deeply into the lip, and during hauling the rope saws even deeper into it. As a result, while being hauled the victim rises into the depth of the overhang, confronting it as a huge barrier. It can be very important for the members at the edge to mitigate this, with either of a couple of different tricks.

First of all, you can slide an ice ax shaft under the rope and push it out to the lip. If the victim is hanging free, you won't be able to push the ax out any farther than the rope already runs. But if there's little or no tension on the rope you should push the ax out as far as the lip will assuredly bear.

If the edge slopes one way or another, then during hauling the rope will slide down the ax shaft. To keep it from sliding off the shaft, place the ax with the adz skyward and on the downhill side of the slope. This way the rope will slide down the shaft to the crotch of the adz and remain there. (Some axes have a sharp edge along this adz-shaft joint and should not be used this way.)

Finally, you should tether the ice ax "pad" to another

ax or anchor of some sort away from the lip (see fig. 3.14), for if the ax falls it invariably falls on the victim. If there's no ax to spare, then a thick cluster of tent poles, a pack, or other items can serve as pads or pad anchors. Ski poles can anchor a pad, but they aren't strong enough to serve as a pad themselves, and if they do break, their ragged broken edges can slice a rope.

If from the fall the rope has already cut too deeply into the lip, the team might have to take a more drastic measure: send down a "fresh" rope over a prepared and prepadded edge. This is discussed on page 119.

Figure 3.14   Padding a crevasse lip (note self-belay
                and backup)

HAULING

With the lip problem prepared for one way or another, the final step before setting up a hauling system is to make sure that the anchor system is adequate. Most hauling systems multiply the force on the anchor just as they multiply the hauling force on their load, because they depend on creating a tension between anchor and load. The force on the hauling anchor will equal the weight of the victim and his gear, plus the friction and resistance at the crevasse lip, multiplied by the pulley system. This is especially dangerous if the victim comes up against the crevasse lip and the haulers continue to pull with all their might; with a pulley system they can generate a tremendous force on the anchor. Therefore, any anchor to be hauled on should be "bombproof."

Once the victim is attached via a prussik to a bombproof anchor, you're ready to set up a hauling system. The most common system is the three-to-one or "Z system." The Z system runs the rope through a pulley at the anchor, then up and back through a second pulley attached to the main rope. Essentially it's a C system except that the rope, instead of tying into the anchor, runs through the anchor and down to the load. When hauling on this system, the haulers pull in 3 feet of rope for every foot that the victim rises, and therefore they have to pull with a force equal to only one-third of the victim's weight, not counting friction. Set up the Z system like this:

1. "Above" the anchor prussik (that is, on the side away from the victim), thread the rope through a belay plate. Known as an "autoblock," this arrangement keeps the anchor prussik from dragging into the pulley you'll put at the anchor. With an autoblock, the anchoring prussik becomes a *ratchet* prussik, allowing the haulers to pull the rope through the system, but stopping the rope from sliding back—and the victim from *falling* back. When the rope is hauled through the pulley, the prussik jams against

the plate and lets the rope run freely; when the rope lets out, the prussik stretches tight and reanchors it.

2. Immediately "above" the autoblock, thread the rope through a pulley, and with a new carabiner clip this pulley into the anchor (see fig. 3.15a).

3. From this pulley at the anchor, loop the rope back parallel to itself as far up toward the crevasse as it's safe to go, and thread the slack line through another pulley.

4. Wrap and set a prussik around the main strand.

5. Clip the new pulley into the new prussik (see fig. 3.15b), and run the slack line back to the anchor. This is the line you haul with, and you're now ready to haul (fig. 3.15c).

▶──────────────────────────────◀

HAULING RATCHETS

There are a number of other methods for creating a ratchet at the anchor in a hauling system, all with advantages and disadvantages. Among the useful ones are the Guarda hitch, the Penberthy knot, and the French braid. I won't attempt to describe these alternatives, but for those who might be introduced to them I will compare their important features.

The Guarda has the advantage of offering an immediate brake, with no slack. However, because no pulley is used it generates added friction. Also, it's easy to forget its simple but crucial construction.

The Penberthy knot and the French braid both offer fairly quick brakes as well, but only slightly or no better than a prussik with an autoblock. Depending on the pulley and perlon used and the tying method, these two ratchet systems can jam into the pulley, adding significant friction or dangerously stopping the pulley.

Because the prussik-autoblock setup offers a system that is easily remembered, is already half-built once a victim is anchored off, and adds almost no friction and only

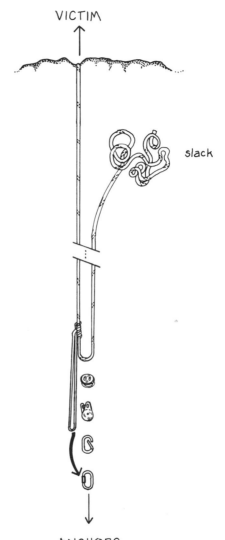

Figure 3.15a Z system for hauling: thread rope through sticht plate (autoblock), then pulley; then clip pulley to anchor (note: prussik is already taut to anchor carabiner, holding weight of victim)

VICTIM

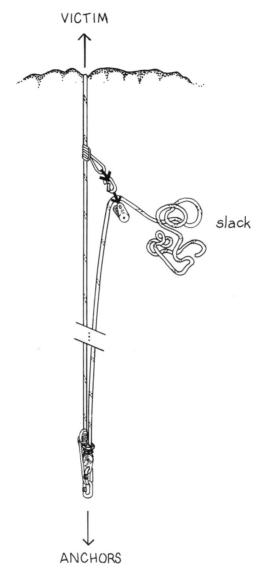

slack

ANCHORS

Figure 3.15b   Z system for hauling: wrap prussik on
loaded line; then thread slack through
pulley and clip to prussik

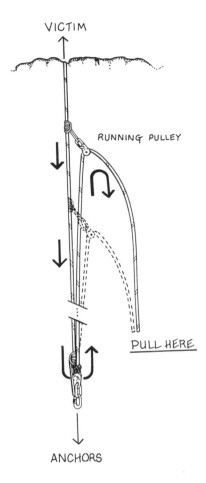

VICTIM

RUNNING PULLEY

PULL HERE

ANCHORS

Figure 3.15c   Z system for hauling: ready to haul

slightly more braking slack (depending on the length of the prussik), most people who experiment with various methods return to this one.

There exists a "prussik-minding" pulley with flanges that keep a prussik away from the wheel, an integral autoblock. A pulley with a rescue-strength cam that will preclude the need for a ratchet prussik is in the design stages.

▶───────────────────────────◀

Hauling itself is a straightforward matter of pulling on the free strand of the rope, in line with the anchor and victim. Added security and power can come from the haulers tying into the rope and pulling from their harnesses, rather than just holding the rope in their hands.

During hauling, the second or "running" pulley moves toward the anchor pulley. Depending on how far the victim needs to be hauled and how far you set the running pulley out from the anchor, you'll probably bring this running pulley up to the anchor. At this point you need to carefully let the victim's weight back onto the ratchet prussik, perhaps stretching out this prussik manually to make doubly sure it immediately grabs.

Here it also doesn't hurt to check that the ratchet prussik isn't getting significantly abraded from the haul rope. In rare cases, mainly on an icy ablation zone where grit can coat the rope, the ratchet prussik can abrade quickly. Once the victim's weight is securely held by the ratchet prussik, you can slide the running pulley and its prussik back down the taut primary rope as far as is practical, and then resume hauling.

As the victim approaches an overhanging lip it's imperative that the haulers slow down, then stop hauling before heaving the victim into the lip. It's surprisingly easy to haul a victim into an overhang, embedding him or her there as a human fluke. Assuming the ratchet prussik holds as tightly as it should, the victim will then be in a very serious predicament, with no reasonable way to move up or down. On one rescue in Alaska, a large party hauled their victim against the overhang with enough force to break her harness, bringing tragedy to what otherwise might have been a successful rescue.

To haul around a lip requires coordination between haulers and victim, for the victim will have to knock away the lip and push away from it; only then can the haulers heave another foot or two. In this way a team hauls around and over a lip in small increments. Of course, this takes communication between the haulers and the victim, and for this reason it's best if a surface member remains at the lip to relay signals. If there's no spare rope for the relayer to tie to the main anchor with, he can set a personal anchor a short distance away from the lip. A less ideal but workable option is for the relayer to simply keep his waist prussik on the haul rope, as a self-belay. If no relayer can be spared, then the haulers must be extremely wary of any increase in the resistance as they haul, and must yell back and forth with the victim as best they can. In chapter 4, the section "Building a Tension Release Mechanism" describes a system that allows a victim to be lowered from implantation into an overhang.

Here's a summary of the bare minimum of gear used to set up the Z system:

2 prussiks or mechanical ascenders
2 anchors
2 pulleys
1, preferably 2 ice axes
1 long runner
6 or 7 carabiners

Therefore, to account for gear that will go into a crevasse with a victim, a party of three should carry at least 50 percent more of each of these items, equally distributed among the members. Parties on glaciers with more serious crevasse hazards are wise to carry more anchors, runners and carabiners. The latter two can be most valuable, for they allow a team to bury and equalize deadman anchors from almost anything, and runners can also substitute for prussiks when tied in a kleimheist knot (see appendix 2). If the team is in a pinch for pulleys, the rope can simply be looped through carabiners instead, but of course the greater friction makes hauling much more difficult. There will be a bit less friction if two carabiners are used in place of any one pulley.

LOWERING A VICTIM WITH THE HAULING SYSTEM

There can be reasons to lower a victim deeper into a crevasse, most obviously if lowering gets the victim to where he can walk or climb out of the crevasse. Another reason is to lower a victim onto a fresh strand, which is described in "Rescuing Over a Newly Prepared Lip," in chapter 4. The key step in lowering a victim is temporarily deactivating the ratchet prussik (or ascender) at the anchor. This requires that you haul the victim up a short distance, and then carefully let rope out through the haul system. The procedure runs as follows:

1. Build a Z system as described above, and then haul the victim just enough to take all the weight off the ratchet prussik.

2. One surface member must hold the wraps of the ratchet prussik open, while another can lower the victim by slowly letting rope out through the haul system. (Both can be done by one person, if necessary.)

3. If the victim needs to be lowered a fair distance, make sure the running pulley of the Z system doesn't run too far away. When this pulley has run a reasonable distance, the rescuer at the anchor resets the ratchet prussik. Then the lowering rescuer can go out to retrieve the running pulley and slide it back close to the anchor. This procedure can be repeated to lower the victim as far as there is free rope.

MIDDLE PERSON IN

Contrary to what one might think, a climber in the middle of a rope team can fall a good distance into a crevasse.

Even though a middle person has a rope on both sides, it's easy for both ropes to be slack or oblique to crevasses. And rescuing a middle person actually can be more problematic.

When a person in the interior of a four-person rope team breaks through a snowbridge, the two surface members who are together on one side of the crevasse can best carry out the rescue. Their procedures are the same as when a member on the end of a three-person rope goes in; the adjacent member holds the weight and the end member sets an anchor "below" them.

However, when the middle person on a three-person team falls into a crevasse, the two end members must hold the fall and then shout back and forth across the crevasse to decide which of them is holding most of the weight. The procedure then runs as follows:

1. The free member goes toward the victim on a self-belay, preferably coming far enough to generate adequate slack to reach the victim.

2. He then sets an anchor and connects it to the rope with a prussik.

3. Next he travels on a self-belay to the crevasse edge, to pad the lip under the rope.

4. Now the weight-bearing member across the crevasse eases toward the victim, letting the weight swing onto his cohort's anchor.

5. The member at the lip who set the anchor can now initiate the rescue, if necessary sending the slack rope down to haul the victim's pack, waiting to assist the prussiking victim over the lip, or setting up a pulley system to haul the victim out (see fig. 3.16).

OTHER HAULING SYSTEMS

For hauling crevasse victims, the Z system has proven to be the most versatile, and in most cases it should be the method of first choice. In fact, knowing more ways to

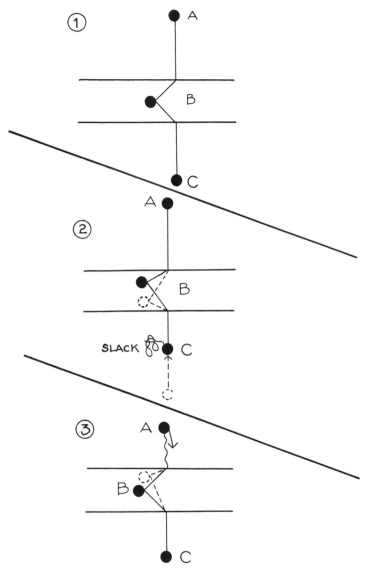

Figure 3.16   Middle person in, schematic sequence: *top*, B falls in; *middle*, A holds weight, C sets anchor, generating slack; *bottom*, A releases B onto anchor, C rescues.

haul can be a burden because in a tense situation rescuers can spend valuable time deciding which method to use, and different methods can even be confused with one another. However, the following two methods can, in the cases mentioned, offer a faster rescue.

STRAIGHT PULL When there are perhaps five or more rescuers available, and the lip is not problematic or has been well prepared, rescuers can usually just directly haul the victim out. Those hauling should either tie into the rope or pull with a prussik or ascender from their harnesses, to make sure that they don't drop the victim. One member must be ready to remove the anchor prussik once the haulers take the victim's weight, and to perhaps replace that prussik should there be a lip problem or other delay.

C PULLEY The simple two-to-one pulley system used to describe pulley theory earlier in this chapter can also be used to haul a victim.

1. Assuming the victim's rope is anchored off with a prussik, thread the slack rope "above" the prussik through a pulley.

2. Clip a carabiner, preferably a locking model, into this pulley. Send the pulley and carabiner to the victim on a loop of rope, holding on to the slack end of the rope.

3. After the victim clips the pulley with its loop of rope to his harness, begin to haul on the end you have been holding onto.

This system is good for a quick and easy haul when the victim is just a few feet into the crevasse, but unable to heave out. This is a common situation, when victims get stuck in a partially collapsed bridge or get wedged between crevasse walls. This system strains the anchor much less than does a Z system, because the friction at the lip bears mostly on the haulers' strand. A disadvantage of the C system is that it can't easily be rigged with a ratcheting belay.

Another system that has long been assumed to work

is the "bilgeri." This system involves running a rope to each of the victim's feet, with both ropes connected to a surface anchor with a prussik. In theory, the victim shifts his weight to one rope while the rescuer pulls up on the other, and by alternating ropes this way the victim reaches the surface. In practice, however, rope stretch and spinning make the bilgeri system impractical.

HYPOTHERMIC VICTIMS

During a prolonged rescue, a crevasse victim often becomes severely chilled, or hypothermic. This condition is not unlike shock. It begins when, in response to cold, the body shunts blood away from the periphery and sequesters it for the internal organs. With prolonged cold even the body's core cools down, and this changes the blood chemistry, drops the metabolism, and generally compromises the organs, especially the heart. A severely hypothermic victim is at great risk of heart failure, especially from jostling of the heart. More than one crevasse victim has died upon reaching the surface and apparent safety, for mysterious but probably related reasons.

Rescuers should thus take whatever care they can to avoid jarring the victim. Once the victim is out of the crevasse, minimize stress and preserve what little blood flow to the organs there is. Immediately lay the victim down and elevate his feet. Then take care to rewarm him gradually. If he can drink, warm fluids can be very helpful, but the most effective treatment is insulated warm (not hot) water bottles around the torso, or the old body-to-body contact in a sleeping bag.

Of course, the best solution is to prevent hypothermia in the first place. The seriousness of getting too cold is a good incentive to have clothing handy, and to have rescue procedures down pat.

C H A P T E R 4

ADDITIONAL RESCUE TECHNIQUES

F or those new to mountain rescue techniques, it's usually challenging enough to first learn the procedural outline of crevasse rescue, and the basic methods described in chapter 3. However, crevasse rescues can demand more than what those basic techniques can accomplish. Therefore, this chapter advances a rescuer's repertoire with techniques designed to prevent or solve complex crevasse-rescue problems, techniques that integrate into the basic procedures of the previous chapter.

Additional Hauling Power

The three-to-one Z system typically requires at least two and often three haulers to get one person out of a crevasse, depending on their strength, the victim's weight, and, es-

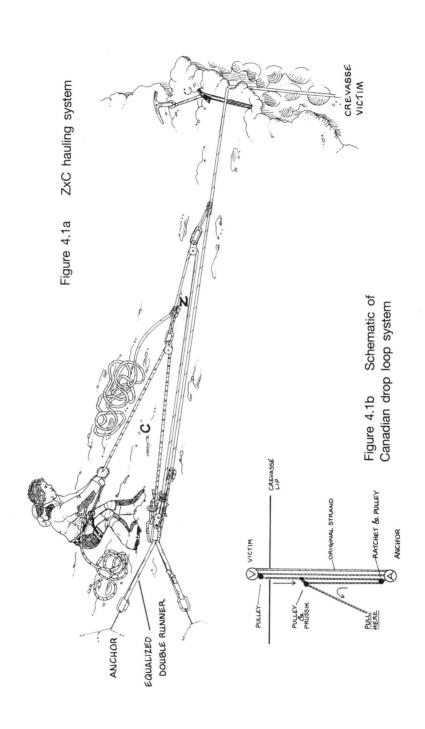

Figure 4.1a   ZxC hauling system

CREVASSE
VICTIM

N

C

ANCHOR

EQUALIZED
DOUBLE RUNNER

Figure 4.1b   Schematic of
Canadian drop loop system

VICTIM

CREVASSE
LIP

ORIGINAL STRAND

RATCHET & PULLEY

ANCHOR

PULLEY

PULLEY
&
PRUSSIK

PULL
HERE

pecially, the amount of friction at the lip. If for any reason you need more hauling power, you can most easily get it by adding a two-to-one C system onto the Z. The fairly simple procedure goes like this:

1. Take the free end of the rope coming off the Z system (or the end of an entirely new rope) and fix it to the anchor.

2. Wrap a prussik on the main hauling line of the Z system just "above" the running pulley.

3. Feed the newly tied line through a pulley and clip this pulley to the new prussik. Bring the line back toward the anchor, and you're ready to haul again on this strand (see fig. 4.1a).

The two-to-one C-pulley subsystem doubles the Z's mechanical advantage to six to one; invariably this is enough for one person to haul out even a heavy victim. Hauling with this system goes slowly, for the victim's strand comes in only one-sixth as fast as the haulers take in rope. The third pulley is a second running pulley, and it will come up against the anchor and have to be reset twice as often as the Z's original running pulley.

Canadian Drop Loop System

Guides and rescue teams in Canada often favor this variation of the 6:1 haul system because tests shows it exerts 40 percent less force on the anchor. The disadvantage is that the victim must be conscious and accessible to a rope throw.

Start building the system by sending a loop of rope from the anchor down to the victim; the victim clips the loop into a pulley and attaches this to his harness. Now you run the strand coming back from the victim through an autoblock and ratchet at the anchor. Run the rope back toward the victim and through a pulley with a prussik on the strand coming up from him, and you're ready to haul. Essentially you've built a Z-system onto a C-system on the victim (see fig. 4.1b).

This system requires more rope, so if only one rope is available the rescuer who sets the anchor will want to set it a good distance "below" the rescuer holding the victim, to generate extra slack. Parties of two with only one rope will generally not have enough rope to build this system.

Building in a Tension Release Mechanism

A tension release mechanism allows rescuers to lower a victim, which several different situations can call for. Most simply, some crevasses allow victims to walk or climb out, once they are lowered to the "floor." More critically, if a victim is inadvertently hauled into a crevasse's overhang, it can be crucial to lower him enough to clear the overhang.

Figure 4.2   Münter hitch

A third reason to lower a victim is to transfer his weight onto a new rope, to circumvent a blocking overhang.

The basic concept of the tension release mechanism is, when anchoring off the victim, not to simply fix the anchoring prussik to the anchor with a carabiner, but to extend the prussik and wrap this extension through a friction brake. The most compact friction brake to use here is a Münter hitch (fig. 4.2), which is then tied off. The procedure described here fits into "Anchoring a Rope," in chapter 3, when a rescuer is ready to connect the victim's rope to an anchor with a prussik:

1. Clip a locking carabiner (preferably a large "Münter 'biner") into the anchor, and wrap a prussik on the victim's rope.

2. Extend the prussik, with a length of either perlon or webbing (see fig. 4.3a). This extension should be at

ANCHOR

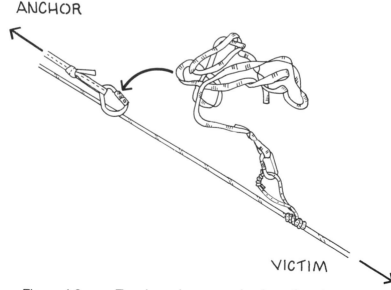

VICTIM

Figure 4.3a   Tension release mechanism: tie extension to new carabiner in a Münter hitch

least 15 feet long. You can either clip or tie it to the prussik, but it must not include any knots along its length. Many guides carry a 40-foot length of 6-millimeter perlon tied in a huge loop to serve as both the prussik and, still doubled, its extension.

3. Tie the extension in a Münter hitch through the locking carabiner. Next, tie off the Münter hitch with a half hitch (fig. 4.3b), and then an overhand knot (full hitch) (fig. 4.3c). As a final backup, knot the very end of the extension and clip it to the anchor (fig. 4.3d).

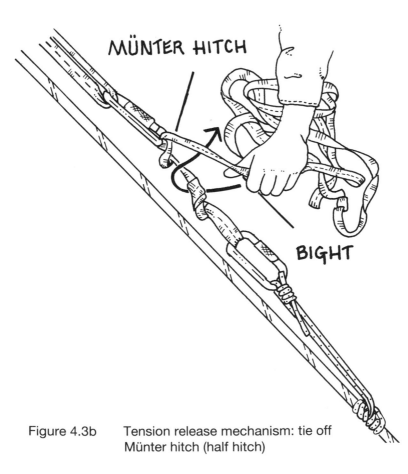

Figure 4.3b   Tension release mechanism: tie off
Münter hitch (half hitch)

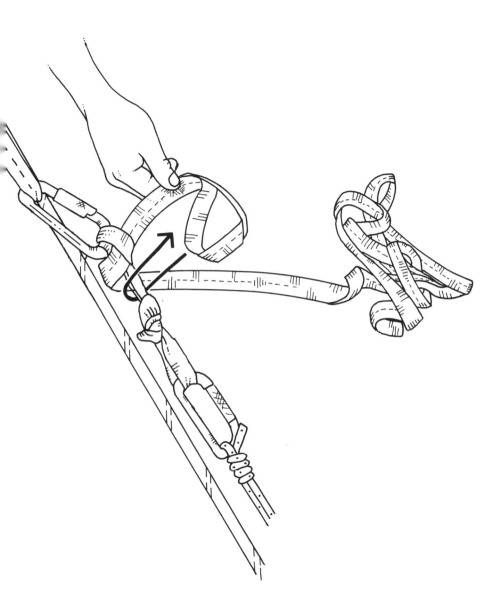

Figure 4.3c   Tension release mechanism: tie off
Münter hitch (full hitch)

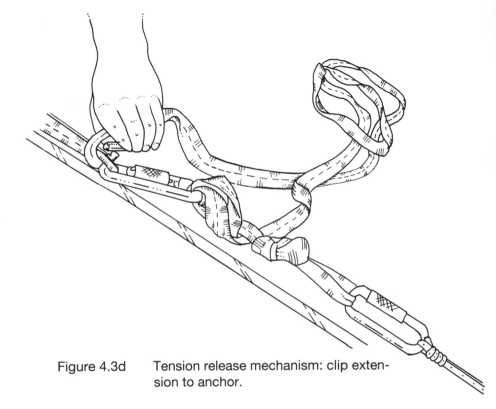

Figure 4.3d   Tension release mechanism: clip extension to anchor.

4. Now you can proceed with the rescue as previously described, and the rescuer holding the victim can release the load onto the Münter hitch and anchor. To set up a hauling system, start with another carabiner on the anchor, and clip the pulley with its autoblock and the rope into this.

5. To lower the victim, undo the full hitch and, while holding firm on the extension, pull out the half hitch. Now you can carefully let out the Münter, which will lower the victim. The Münter hitch is a high-friction brake, and lowering a victim over a crevasse lip will not be a problem. When the victim is lowered far enough, retie the half and full hitches.

6. For hauling, you'll probably want to get the anchor (ratchet) prussik back close to the anchor before retying the hitches. To do this, have others (if available) hold the victim's weight via the haul system while you slide the ratchet prussik back and pull the extension back through the Münter, and then retie the backup knots. With the anchor prussik back near the anchor, you can lower the victim again if necessary.

A tension release mechanism can be added into a haul system even if you have fixed the original anchoring prussik to the anchor, as described earlier. To do this, wrap a new ratchet prussik onto the victim's strand and add the Münter extension onto a fresh (locking) carabiner at the anchor. Build the haul system and haul just enough to take the weight off the original prussik, which you can then unclip and remove. Now the tension release prussik is also the main ratchet prussik.

To those who are relatively new to rescue techniques, building a tension release mechanism can seem a complicated and confusing addition. Indeed, it is not worth doing and dangerous to attempt if the rescuers don't understand the principles and know the procedure well. However, for those with experience, the tension release mechanism simply inserts a proven belay into the victim's anchor attachment, and with practice the mechanism can be added in less than half a minute.

Rescuing Over a Newly Prepared Lip

As has been emphasized, during a crevasse fall the rope can cut very deeply into the lip, and getting the victim past a great eave can pose a major obstacle. The surest way to solve the problem is by sending down a "fresh" rope over a prepared and prepadded edge, to the side of where the original rope has cut in. However, in clearing away a large overhang great care has to be taken to avoid bombarding the victim with blocks of snow. The surface member who goes out to check the victim should decide if cultivating a new edge is necessary. If it is, the procedure then goes as follows:

1. Build a Z or ZxC haul system on the victim's original rope and haul him to within a few feet of the overhang. This gets the victim out of the way of falling debris, and generates more slack.

2. To the side of the original rope, far enough away to keep the victim clear, knock away the lip and set a rope pad, as described in "Preparing Crevasse Lips" in chapter 3.

3. Send the "fresh" strand of rope down for the victim to tie into, and then run it over the newly prepared lip site. It will be easier to use an entirely different rope if one is available, although sending down the other end of the victim's original strand works fine if it's your only rope.

4. Connect the fresh strand to the anchor with a prussik, and pull the slack out of the rope and prussik.

5. On the original haul line, lower the victim until his weight swings onto the new strand, using one of two methods. As described earlier, you can lower with the original haul system. Alternatively, if you have built a tension release hitch into your ratchet prussik, you can untie the backup hitches and lower the victim out with the Münter hitch.

6. Using the newly weighted strand, either the victim can ascend out of the crevasse, or surface members can haul him out by breaking down the original haul system and building a new one on the fresh strand. Once the victim's weight is completely off the original strand, the victim should untie from it, to avoid getting it snagged in the overhang.

Two-person Parties

As mentioned before, traveling on a glacier with just one partner begets the serious possibility of one person rescuing another. For this reason the traditional wisdom has been "never travel with fewer than three." But for many people, this is too restricting. Indeed, many parties travel across glaciers in order to reach a technical climb, where the most efficient team will be a pair. Also, it can be hard enough to gather even one partner with the time, ability and interest to take a trip, much less two or more. But while the incentives tempting one to go onto a glacier with just one partner are clear, they make it easy to overlook the central question: do pairs really have the "safety net"— the backup of rescue—that they need?

A party of two *can* have a reasonable safety net if they are cautious about the crevasses they cross, and if they are very competent at rescue technique. In fact, it can be safer to travel with one competent partner than with any number of incompetent ones. However, while one competent individual can perform most crevasse rescue procedures, roped pairs need to understand that the most basic element of initiating a crevasse rescue can be very difficult for *any* one person: setting an anchor.

When one climber holds a partner's crevasse fall, very often the partner's weight continues to bear. It's while holding this weight (mitigated by friction of the rope over the crevasse lip) that the surface member must set an anchor. Too few glacier travelers have given much thought to the need to set an anchor while holding a person's weight, much less practiced it. But imagine holding your partner's crevasse fall and *not* anchoring off. Do you just lie there in self-arrest and hope he can prussik out, while both your lives depend on your grip in the snow? How long do you wait?

Pairs should keep at least two anchors appropriate to the conditions very handy, ideally clipped to their harnesses or low on their packs' shoulder straps. They should also, of course, have prussiks on the rope (or ascenders *very* handy), for these are what will connect the taut rope to the anchor. Remember, too, that each partner should travel with enough slack rope to reach the other. Assume now the worst case, in which you've had to hold a fall with a self-arrest. From here your procedure goes as follows:

1. Work from the self-arrest position to a position that allows you to still hold the victim's weight but free at least one hand to set an anchor. Usually the key is to dig in your feet and bear as much of the load with them as possible. One good compromise position is to roll onto one leg and brace with the other, perhaps still holding onto the ice ax. The pose looks something like a baseball player classically sliding into home plate (see fig. 4.4). If the victim's weight bears heavily, you might have to stay generally prone in self-arrest.

2. Assuming the anchor of choice is a fluke, scour out a T-shaped trench, as similar as possible to the ideal trench described in "Anchors" in chapter 3. If you've been successful at taking most of the weight with your feet, you might be able to dig with your ice ax. Otherwise, you'll have to dig with your hand or perhaps a second ice tool. Gauge the site of the trench so that when you set the fluke, the extensions of your prussiks or ascenders will just reach the fluke's carabiner. If you've been traveling with a Texas prussik system on the rope, dig the fluke's trench at about shoulder level, and the stirrup loops should barely reach the fluke's carabiner.

3. Set the fluke and give it test yanks.

4. Connect the fluke to the rope with a prussik or ascender. Here we see another bonus of traveling with the Texas system on the rope, for the stirrup loops can be pulled out and immediately clipped to the fluke.

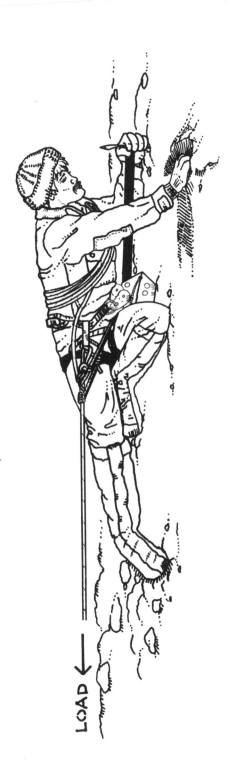

Figure 4.4　Lone rescuer setting an anchor

5. Ease back toward the crevasse, keeping a watchful eye on the fluke. As you back away, the victim's weight transfers onto the fluke. Be ready to jump back into self-arrest should this primary anchor fail.

6. When the primary anchor obviously holds all the victim's weight, unclip from the rope and add a backup anchor (as described in "Backing Up," in chapter 3). Make sure there's a minimum of slack in the connecting runner.

With the rope anchored off, rescue procedures are the same as for larger parties, except there are fewer options.

7. With a self-belay on the slack rope you've been carrying, go to the lip and check your buddy's condition. If he needs his pack hauled, you can send down the remaining free rope and yank it up hand over hand. If he can then ascend out on his own, you can wait at the lip to help heave him over it. If he absolutely needs your assistance to be freed or for first aid, then you can pad the lip and go down immediately, taking the necessary clothing and gear.

8. If your partner needs to be hauled, do what you can to prepare the lip under his rope without bombarding him with blocks of snow.

9. Go back to your anchors and build a six-to-one (ZxC) pulley system, preferably with a tension-release hitch. While hauling, remain very sensitive to any increase in resistance, because of course there's no one to relay warnings when your buddy is coming to an overhang, and if he's injured there's no one to assist him over. When you do feel added resistance, stop hauling and give your buddy a chance to knock away an eave or push away from it.

10. When you suspect you've pulled your partner up to the final lip, it's wise to run out to the edge and make sure you're going to be able to haul over it. Go out on a self-belay set on the main rescue line. You might need to carefully knock away as much of the overhang as possible

now; with your partner close to the lip, it will be safer to knock away hunks of snow. How much of a lip you can haul over depends on how capable the victim is to help himself, and how deeply the rope cuts into the lip.

11. Once the lip is certainly surmountable, return to the haul system and heave your buddy up.

If the rope knifes very deeply into the lip, and/or if the victim is too injured to help much, you might have to haul over a new site to the side. Without rescue partners this is difficult, but without someone at the lip to help an incapacitated victim, hauling over even a small eave can prove impossible. The new-site procedure is basically the same as when there are two or more rescuers:

1. When you've hauled to near the final overhang, put a self-belay on the free strand of rope, and go out to the lip. To the side of where your buddy dangles, prepare the new haul site.

2. Send down the free end of the rope for your partner to tie into, and then run the strand over the newly prepared site.

3. Go back to the haul system and anchor off the "new" strand with a prussik, pulling all the slack out of this strand.

4. Then lower the victim so his weight comes fully onto the new strand. If you rigged your haul system with a tension-release hitch, you can probably lower out enough with this. If not, you can lower with the haul system as described on page 106, holding the ratchet prussik open yourself.

5. Break down the first haul system and build a new one on the fresh strand. Now you're ready to haul over the freshly prepared site.

Clearly, with a lone rescuer the rescue for any crevasse fall is both involved and uncertain; thus two-person parties should travel and cross crevasses more conservatively than a larger group might. Pairs should realize that even if they are practiced at rescue procedures, setting an anchor and hauling past a large lip are weak strands in their safety net. Of course each member of a pair needs to carry enough gear to rescue the other—at least two anchors for any conditions expected, preferably three pulleys, and also extra runners, carabiners and prussiks.

TYING OFF A BELAY (SLIP HITCH)

When members of a two-person party decide to belay across a fragile-looking crevasse bridge, and the bridge does indeed fail, the belayer will have to "tie off" the belay. With hands then freed, the rescuer can anchor off the rope. The tie-off knot is the same as described for the Münter tie-off. Assuming you hold the fall with a sticht plate in a sitting anchored belay, here's the general procedure. Depending on the harness, you may need to tie the hitches "above" the belay plate, around the loaded strand.

1. With one hand, hold the rope back from the belay plate to maintain the friction that holds the victim's weight. With the free hand bring a bight of rope from the brake hand around the harness loop, and pass the bight under the loop created (fig. 4.5a). This is the tie-off half hitch.

2. Still holding the brake strand, pull plenty of slack into the bight, and pull out all of the slack between the brake hand and the bight. Hold onto the bight and let go with the brake hand. The weight of the victim will tighten the half hitch (fig. 4.5b).

3. Tie the bight around the harness strand in a whole hitch, the tie-off backup (fig. 4.5c).

4. Now you are free to connect the rope to the anchor, as in any crevasse rescue situation. Wrap a prussik around the load rope and clip the prussik to the anchor. Ease toward the victim, letting his weight come onto the prussik and anchor. Now you can untie the hitches at your harness and carry out a rescue.

CLIMBER

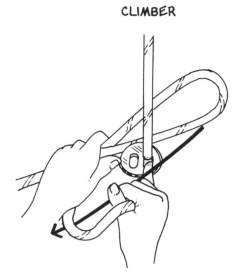

Figure 4.5a Tying off a belay: hold belay and tie a half hitch around harness loop.

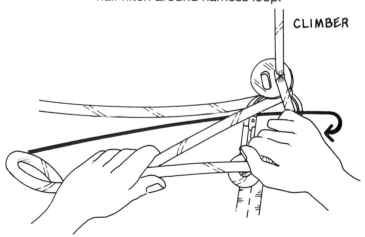

Figure 4.5b Tying off a belay: pull out slack between brake hand and half hitch.

CLIMBER

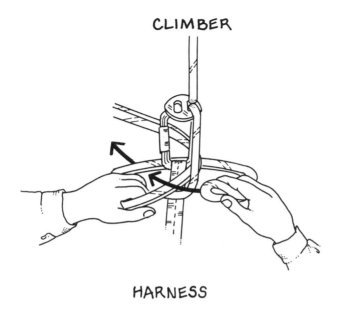

HARNESS

Figure 4.5c   Tying off a belay: tie bight around
harness loop in whole hitch.

Rappelling to Aid a Victim

What do you do when you go out to the crevasse lip and there's a labored, pained response, or no response? Is the victim hanging limp? Is he wearing a pack? A chest harness? Can you even see him? Do you go down to help? If the victim is severely injured, severely hypothermic or unconscious, going down could be the only way to save his life. On the other hand, the time it takes for someone to go down and administer to a victim suffering only slightly can be time enough to have them suffering severely, and putting a second person in a crevasse is not to be taken lightly. Decisions like these cannot be covered with blanket statements, and in rescue situations often too little is known to say with certainty that a given decision will be the right one.

To help, it's important to know what conditions can put a crevasse victim in mortal danger. Hypothermia is probably the most common trauma that crevasse rescuers can do much about. Severe bleeding is another case in which rescuers might save a person's life by going down immediately. More mechanically, victims often get wedged between crevasse walls or set in snow, and need help getting free. A problem most inherent to vertical rescues arises when a victim hangs unconsciously, because typically his lax tongue slumps over his airway, and in this condition a victim likely will suffocate in minutes.

Whatever the reason to go down, in rescue terminology the person going down to aid the victim is the "third man." It's preferable for the third man to go down on a completely fresh rope, keeping the slack part of the victim's rope available for a hauling system. But let's assume a three-person party with only one rope:

1. With luck the victim's strand was originally anchored as much as 15 to 20 feet down from the rope's center, for this will allow enough slack both to build a Z-pulley system and to rappel on. The anchor should be backed up for a second person's weight.

2. Tie the rappel strand to the anchor not quite 15 feet along the slack side from the rope's center (here it pays to have the middle of your rope marked). This should leave you enough rope to reach the victim, and about 30 to 40 feet of slack to set up a Z hauling system on the victim's strand.

3. Gather the supplies you'll need for administering first aid, keeping the victim and you warm, and chopping or digging out the victim, as well as slings and prussiks for rigging support, as described below. Don't forget prussiks or ascenders to get yourself back out!

4. Go to the lip, to the side where the victim's rope

disappears, and prepare a site to rappel over.

5. Wrap a prussik around the rappel strand and clip it to your harness. This will be your brake upon reaching the victim. As you rappel, hold the prussik wraps open, bringing the prussik down with you.

6. As you rappel to just barely above the victim, halt your rappel by letting go of the prussik wraps and settling onto the prussik.

7. Take off the victim's pack and clip it out of the way. Administer first aid, free the victim from wedging or snow burial, or whatever else needs to be done.

8. Tell your partner on the surface to set up a haul system and prepare to haul.

9. Ascend with the victim as your partner proceeds to haul him up.

This basic sequence of "third man" procedures has omitted the most technical consideration, because it deserves a discussion of its own: making sure that the victim, especially if unconscious or semiconscious, hangs with his head upright, and as comfortably as possible. Here the third man's crucial job is to rig support for the victim's torso and head, keeping the head tilted back to keep the airway open. A conscious but badly injured victim or a hypothermic victim who might go unconscious should be given this support during a rescue. However, even an experienced climber will need practice to get this procedure down:

1. As you hang off a waist-prussik just above the victim, rig a chest harness on the victim (fig. 4.6a).

2. Put a prussik or ascender on the rope the victim hangs from.

3. Clip a runner to the prussik and run this through a carabiner on the chest harness; this carabiner then acts as an improvised C pulley, and you can raise the victim's torso by pulling the runner back up to the prussik (fig. 4.6b). (Without this "pulley" it will be virtually impossible to raise

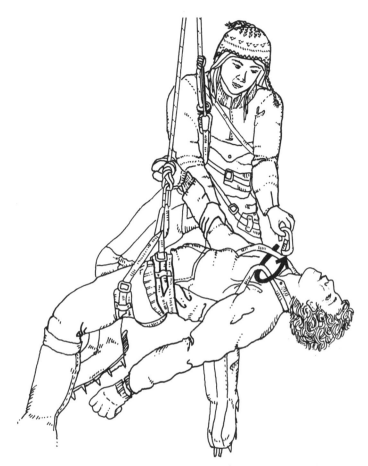

Figure 4.6a   Improvising support for an unconscious
victim: rigging a chest harness

the victim's torso.) Set the prussik so that the victim's
torso will hang from it at a slight incline, and then clip
this other end of the runner into the prussik.

4. With another runner padded by an article of clothing,
support the victim's nape and head, clipping this runner
to another prussik or perhaps the same one as for the chest
harness. Make sure the victim's head is supported but tilted
back, to keep the airway open.

Figure 4.6b   Improvising support for an unconscious victim: an improvised C-pulley allows victim's torso to be raised and clipped into supported position.

5. If necessary, support the victim's legs with another prussik and a runner or two (fig. 4.6c).

Clearly, rescuing an unconscious victim is a demanding procedure, and it might never be carried out fast enough

Figure 4.6c   Improvising support for an unconscious victim: use prussik and runner to support victim's legs.

to save a life. Perhaps the most important lesson from this is to emphasize the value of full-body harnesses, and the seriousness of severe crevasse falls. But as "third man" procedures become more widely known, perhaps lives will be saved.

Climber on the Challenger Glacier, the North Cascade
Mountains, Washington

CHAPTER 5

SKIING
AND HAULING
SLEDS

S kis and sleds both allow parties to cover much more ground and carry more weight. But they also throw new factors into glacier travel and crevasse rescue.

Glacier Skiing

Traveling on skis gives the obvious benefit of spreading your body weight over a greater surface area, making you less likely to fall through a given snowbridge. The increase in surface area is about six- to ninefold, although this does not make you six to nine times less likely to fall through. Skis' bridging effectiveness varies with a number of factors, including the direction the skis point relative to the crevasse and what type of snow is present. But clearly skis' greater surface area and greater bridging ability make them a safety item, especially when traveling uphill.

Of course, the joy and real efficiency in skiing come from traveling downhill. And, unfortunately, skiing downhill and safeguarding against crevasse falls are not very compatible. Even the best skiers hold no illusions about trying to link turns while roped to a partner who's trying to do the same, while both are looking out for and avoiding crevasses. Many people try it once, and find out they're more likely to get pulled off into a crevasse than anything else. Therefore, skiing downhill while roped for glacier travel means, at best, skidding along in a measured snowplow, perhaps cutting an occasional christy to change direction. The better skier should ski behind, because he or she adjusts to the pace of the skier ahead to keep a minimum of slack in the rope. To keep the pace slow and stay in control, many people keep their skins on. Skiers should have runaway straps, to keep a released ski from disappearing into a crevasse.

The other problem with skiing in crevassed terrain, uphill or downhill, is holding a fall. When one member crosses a known crevasse, the adjacent member can turn his or her skis sideways to the potential pull, to better resist a fall. But in any serious fall the adjacent member will be pulled off his feet. For this reason, ski poles should be rigged with self-arrest grips. Another option is to wrap an ice ax to one of the poles using duct tape. For getting out of a crevasse, one should make arrangements to remove skis and attach them to the pack.

Some people feel that skis' added surface area makes crevasse falls unlikely enough that they can dispense with a rope. While it's indisputable that skis help, no one can make this judgment absolutely, and it's easy to base the judgment more on a desire to have fun than on the glacier's conditions. On Oregon's Mount Hood, a cohort of mine was linking telemarks down an apparently crevasse-free snow slope, and he carved one right into a covered slot, plunging parallel to the walls for 50 feet. Amazingly, he suffered only minor injuries, and his buddies rescued him.

A party can easily be tempted to ski downhill unroped if they have skied up a glacier as a rope team, checking out the best route and general snowbridge conditions. If everything seems safe enough, they can ski down with more confidence, roping up where prudent. Even with this prior inspection, though, ski parties tend to skew their judgment because once the skis are pointing down, the temptation to value fun over safety can be great. Also, snow-bridges generally weaken as a day progresses, and bridges that seemed fine on the morning climb can fail during the afternoon descent.

Snowshoes also reduce your chances of breaking through a given snowbridge, although their surface area and bridging length are significantly less than skis'. There's no problem controlling a downhill plod with snowshoes, though, so for those less skilled at skiing or who are carrying a large pack or sled, snowshoes can be a smart compromise.

Hauling Sleds

Other than traveling unroped, there's probably nothing a glacier traveler can do to make crevasse falls more dangerous than to simply haul a sled. We might marvel at how much easier it is to haul a 60-pound expedition load on a sled than on a backpack, but in a crevasse fall that sled plunges in right after you, and when the rope brings you to a halt, those 60 pounds plummet onto you with a deadly force. In recent years at least two crevasse deaths on Denali can be partly or largely attributed to sleds.

The basic preventive to sled slayings is to attach the sled to the climbing rope behind you. This way, as the rope comes taut, the sled will halt and stay suspended above you in the crevasse. No perfect system for setting this up

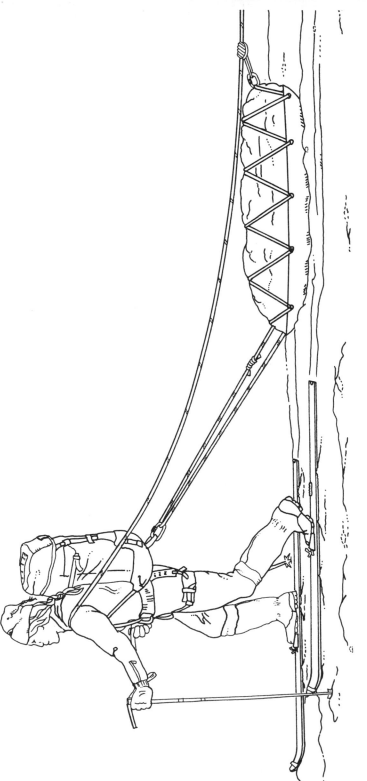

Figure 5.1   Glacier travel with a sled

has yet been devised that offers all the safety and convenience we'd like, but the best system is a pretty good compromise.

Most people on typical budgets get by with the inexpensive plastic sleds designed for kids' snow frolics. While custom expedition sleds with aluminum haul poles are nice, these do not prevent the load crashing onto you. Another good option is to drag a haul bag made of smooth, heavy fabric.

In any case, it's most comfortable to haul a sled with a separate haul line clipped to a carabiner on the back of your pack. Attach the sled to the climbing rope with a three-wrap prussik on the sled's trailing end. Adjust the prussik along the climbing rope so that when you're traveling and the haul rope is taut, the climbing rope has an absolute minimum of slack (see fig. 5.1). You don't want the climbing rope taut so that you're hauling the sled with it, but you also don't want it slack so that you hang from the sled's haul line when you fall through. It's wise to load gear into a duffle and attach the prussik to a strong loop on the duffle, not to the sled's plastic, which could rip under the stress of a fall.

If you have the appropriate minimum of slack in this system, when you do punch through a snowbridge most of your weight goes onto the climbing rope, because the stretch and play in the prussik sink the sled toward you just enough to take tension off the haul line. Thus you hang from your seat harness as without a sled (see fig. 5.2), and when you remove your pack you also detach yourself from the sled.

To ascend out of the crevasse past the sled's prussik, you need a spare prussik (or an ascender that goes on and off the rope easily) and a spare harness carabiner. With the Texas prussik system you simply ascend to the sled's prussik, wrap your spare prussik on the climbing rope above the sled's prussik, stand tall to clip this new prussik into

Figure 5.2   In a crevasse with a sled

your spare locking carabiner, and unclip the original prussik. When you rise up enough to hang from the new waist
prussik, take your feet out of the stirrups and rewrap the
stirrup prussik above the sled's prussik. If you use ascenders, make sure that both ascenders attach to your seat
harness, and when you reach the sled's prussik, replace the
ascenders one at a time above the prussik. If the sled is
heavy, you will need to untie from the climbing rope to
continue. It is best to get a belay from your partners above.

Should a victim with a sled need to be hauled out,
you'll want to send down a new strand to haul on, one
without a sled attached to it. After being hauled a short
distance, the victim can untie from the original rope, and
the sled can be hauled up later.

Another problem with sleds is dragging them downhill and along sidehills, for they slide and roll downslope at
their own whim, paying no heed to their owner's most
fervent demands and sometimes threatening to drag the
owner away. Clipping a sled into the glacier travel rope
can help solve these problems too, for the climber behind
can then help brake and even steer the sled. To aid in this
you can clip clove hitches in the climbing rope in front and
behind the sled, adjusting the hitches so there's slight tension between them across the top of the sled. When de-
scending, the member behind brakes the sled with the climbing rope, keeping it from crashing into the partner's legs.
Another aid for downhill travel is to run a knotted rope
under the sled's belly as a friction brake, tying it at both
bow and stern.

To keep the sled from swinging downslope on a tra-
verse of a sidehill, the member behind keeps tension on
the climbing rope, and, especially with double clove hitches
on the sled, this tension holds the sled in line with the
direction of travel. Though the member ahead is now
pulling against this tension, and coordination between the
two members needs to be close, this is far better than having

the sled slide, flip and pull downslope. Another consideration, though, is that the clove hitches in the climbing rope will be impossible to untie should the rope be tensioned with the weight of someone who's fallen in a crevasse, and this will make it impossible to haul the victim out on that rope. For this reason, it's wise to tie in the sled with clove hitches only when another rope or rope team is available.

You may have noticed that all these precautions and improvements can't be applied to the last person in a rope team, who has no one behind to keep a sled in line. Basically, a team has two unsavory options for the last person. The first is not to give that person a sled (but a heavier pack instead?), and to distribute his load among the other members. The second is to give him a sled but travel very cautiously, clipping the sled to the rope ahead when crossing treacherous bridges.

A F T E R W O R D

THE GAME OF CREVASSE ROULETTE

▶───────────────────────◀

As mentioned in the introduction, a party's style of glacier travel generally reflects its attitudes. People go into glaciated areas pretty sure about how much risk they are willing to take to complete their endeavor. As they perceive various degrees of hazard they adjust their procedures to maintain that acceptable level of risk.

But since the crevasse hazard can never be gauged precisely, glacier travel is always a gamble that a party's precautions will match up with the actual hazard. Not only is it difficult to know just where crevasses lie and how strong their bridges are, it's even harder to predict how severe a crevasse fall might be and what the extrication would involve. Thus, when a party settles on procedures such as the number of rope teams, how to cross what bridges at what time of day, how many anchors to carry and so on, they can't know exactly what they're preparing for. To emphasize this uncertainty, we can think of glacier travel as a kind of crevasse roulette, a game of chance in which the percentage of unlucky turns of the wheel is never sure.

The object of crevasse roulette is to travel on a glacier with the minimum of gear and rigamarole, while keeping the chances of dying in a crevasse as overwhelmingly small as possible.

When confronted with this metaphor for glacier travel, most of us say we'd like to play the game at a fairly conservative level. That is, we like the security of being able to rescue ourselves from the worst-case scenario—falling a good distance into a crevasse to a free-hanging stop, perhaps with injuries. This we want beyond the relative security of knowing we will usually avoid that worst-case scenario in the first place.

A major reason we want such safety is because we see crevasses as an unglamorous risk, not worth tempting fate for—in contrast to, say, scaling a peak. Unfortunately, this same "not worth risking" attitude also too often includes "not worth hassling for." This "nuisance" view of the crevasse hazard dilutes our interest in giving ourselves the safety we're expecting. We rope up but don't carry or don't know how to use anchors or prussiks, we carry heavy packs without chest harnesses, we travel with yards of slack rope between us.

In this way it seems that, because crevasses generally are not impressive hazards inherent to "climbing," and because their odds are irregular and many glacier excursions are free of incidents, we don't see crevasses with the same wary eye as we do other climbing hazards like falling, fatigue or even avalanches and rockfall. We forget that a single crevasse fall can become the major issue of a mountaineering endeavor. With the hazards not well thought out, our perception of playing crevasse roulette at a conservative level becomes a pleasant illusion compared to our real odds.

Most people who have died in crevasses were climbing unroped, and the overwhelming majority of those people were surprised—they were either naive about the risk or they denied the risk they knew. We can guess that most who've died while climbing roped assumed that the precautions they were taking were adequate to save them from the fatal situation. Very few went out fully aware of the risk and fully ready to take it.

This is not to say that we should travel glaciers with the least possible risk—which would be to anchor-belay every step. Our goal is to play crevasse roulette at a level of risk as close to our choosing as possible. When we have an intimate knowledge of and intuition for crevasses and snowbridges, we can play at a more informed, aware level. When we know how to avoid the worst case and how to rescue from it, we can play at whatever level we want, up to the conservative level that most people desire.

We all know that one person's acceptable risk is another's suicide mission, and yet another's confining security blanket; it's important that we preserve this freedom to climb in the style we choose. Just as important is that we accept full responsibility for whatever style we choose. The crucial task is not eliminating risk, but knowing more clearly just what risks we take, and just how effectively our precautions will serve us. Given this knowledge, glacier travelers almost always make prudent choices.

Experienced glacier travelers know the stakes are high, and relative security from crevasse death comes with precious little investment. An experienced party on a typical alpine glacier can be quite secure with just a pound or two of gear they wouldn't carry anyway, and perhaps fifteen minutes of added procedure. Mostly it's weightless, time-free items—awareness and ability—that are our best investments, for in crevasse roulette they both reduce the hassle and improve the odds.

A P P E N D I C E S

1. Rescue Practice Sessions

One of the paradoxes of glacier travel is that safe, uneventful trips do not prepare you for the eventuality of crevasse rescue. Therefore, competence at crevasse rescue demands setting up practice sessions on a glacier.

It's usually more convenient to first practice at a crevasse in a glacier's ablation zone. Here, on the icy lower reaches, you don't have to worry about genuine crevasse falls before you've learned how to rescue people from them, the anchors in ice are safer, and you don't have to worry about genuine lip problems.

First, find a flat area with a nice deep crevasse. Set up bombproof anchors and, with a belay device, lower a mock victim into the crevasse. (The "victim" can be a pack full of gear or snow instead of a person.) He or she (or it) should go down tied to the end of another rope, which will become the rescue/haul rope. Once the victim is a good distance into the crevasse, set another bombproof anchor, pull the rescue rope taut, connect it to the anchor with a prussik, and commence rescue procedures. As you haul the victim up, someone takes up the original lowering rope as a backup belay.

To practice prussiking, have your partner lower you with a brake on the anchor and tie off the belay. Then prussik out on the same rope.

Once your group is practiced at rescue procedures, it's a good idea to head up to the snow-covered reaches of

147

a glacier and practice in more genuine conditions. Here again, choose your practice site carefully; try to find a flat work area next to a good crevasse with at most a modest eave of snow. You don't want to walk onto a huge, unstable marquee that might require the adrenaline of a genuine rescue to get back over. If you're in the Cascades in July or August you should have no problem finding a suitable crevasse, but if you're in the Alaska Range you might just decide to stay out of as many crevasses as possible. Again, set bomb-proof anchors and lower a mock victim, then haul out on another set of anchors.

2. Some Useful Improvisations

Here are three additional tricks that can come in handy.

KIWI COIL TIE-IN

Guides in New Zealand have developed a method for people at the end of a rope to tie in that wraps coils around the shoulder and offers reasonable torso support.

1. Start by tying the end of the rope into your seat harness as usual, then wrap coils from the shoulder and under the other arm. Wrap the coils so they reach just to the bottom of your rib cage (fig. A.1a). If you're at one end of a three- or four-person rope team, wrap about five coils. If you're one of a two-person rope team, wrap enough coils to take up the amount of rope you need to reach your partner (see page 38).

2. When you have enough coils wrapped, make a bight in the rope as it comes from under your arm, and with this tie an overhand knot around all the coils (fig. A.1b).

3. Clip the knotted bight into doubled carabiners on your seat harness. When you hang from this tie-in, most of your weight should bear on the seat harness, with the coils reaching out from your torso somewhat, merely supporting your upper body. Test pull the rope to make sure that the seat harness will take its share of the weight, and re-tie the knot if necessary.

This method shortens the span between climbers and ensures some free rope on the ends, so all the advantages and disadvantages of shorter spans apply. Wearing a pack poses a small problem, however, for a pack should be worn over the coils for easy removal, and if the pack is heavy it carries uncomfortably. Some feel the coils still offer enough support when worn over pack straps.

Figure A.1a   A kiwi coil-tie in: wrap coils around shoulder and under arm.

Figure A.1b   A kiwi coil-tie in: use bight to tie overhand knot around coils.

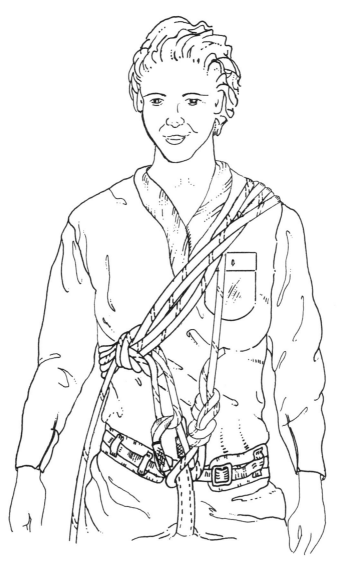

Figure A.1c   A kiwi coil-tie in: clip bight into carabiner
on seat harness.

KLEIMHEIST WEBBING "PRUSSIK"

With a runner of 1-inch or 9/16-inch webbing you can improvise a prussik by tying it around a climbing rope in a *kleimheist* knot. Hold an open bight of the webbing free, and wrap it down the rope barber-pole style, making three to four wraps. Then feed the tail back up through the bight you've held open (fig. A.2a), pull the tail back down, and the kleimheist is complete. This can be used anywhere a prussik is used, except as a ratchet at the anchor of a hauling system.

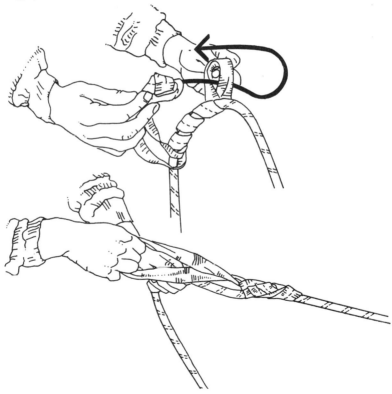

Figure A.2   Kleimheist knot tied with 1-inch webbing: *top*, wrap bight down rope barber pole style; *bottom*, feed tail back through bight.

BACHMAN KNOT

Familiar to Europeans, the Bachman is a prussik-type knot that actually performs better than the tried-and-true prussik. With its wraps cinching around a carabiner's spine as well as the climbing rope, the Bachman grabs at least as tightly as a prussik, yet once the load is removed it slides more readily. The carabiner also adds a convenient handle.

To tie the Bachman, simply clip a "prussik" loop into a carabiner, and then wrap the cord around both the climbing rope and the spine of the carabiner, working down the carabiner barber pole style. Three wraps will usually suffice, depending on the diameter of the rope. When you load the remaining loop, the Bachman grabs; when you push or pull the wraps and 'biner directly, it slides. The Bachman can be used anywhere a prussik would be used.

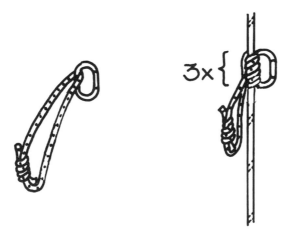

Figure A.3   Bachman knot

Index

155

Andy Selters has climbed all over North America, Mexico, and Asia and is the author of four other mountain guidebooks and numerous mountaineering articles. During his years as a guide and trainer for the American Alpine Institute in Bellingham, Washington, Selters felt the need for updated literature on glacier travel and crevasse rescue, from which this guidebook sprung. He now lives in Bishop, California.